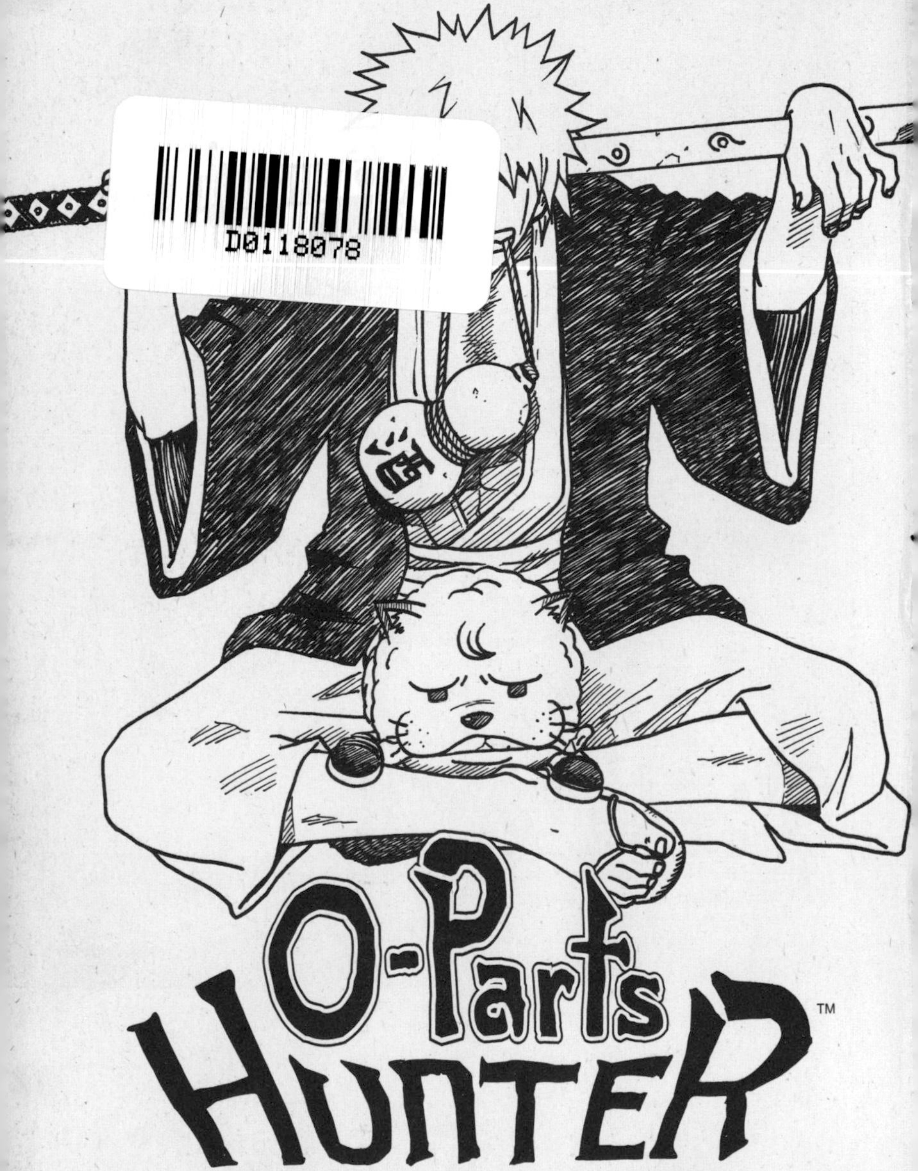

O-Parts HUNTER™

SEISHI KISHIMOTO

LET HIM THAT HATH UNDER-STANDING COUNT THE NUMBER OF THE BEAST: FOR IT IS THE NUMBER OF A MAN; AND HIS NUMBER IS...

666

REVELATION 13:18
A VERSE OUT OF THE *NEW TESTAMENT*

O-Parts Hunter

SPIRITS

O-PARTS

Spirit: A special energy force which only the O.P.T.s have. The amount of Spirit they have within them determines how strong of an O.P.T. they are.

O-Parts: Amazing artifacts with mystical powers left from an ancient civilization. They have been excavated from various ruins around the world. Depending on its Effect, O-Parts are given a rank from E to SS within a seven-tiered system.

Effect: The special energy (power) the O-Parts possess. It can only be used when an O.P.T. sends his Spirit into an O-Part.

O.P.T.: Those who have the ability to release and use the powers of the O-Parts. The name O.P.T. is an abbreviated form of O-Part Tactician.

CHARACTERS

Jio Freed
A wild O.P.T. boy whose dream is world domination! He has been emotionally damaged from his experiences in the past, but is still gung-ho about his new adventures! O-Part: New Zero-shiki (Rank B) Effect: Triple (Increasing power by a factor of three)

Ruby
A treasure hunter who can decipher ancient texts. She meets Jio during her search for a legendary O-Part.

Satan
This demon is thought to be a mutated from of Jio. It is a creature shrouded in mystery with earth-shattering powers.

STORY

Ascald: a world where people fight amongst themselves in order to get their hands on mystical objects left behind by an ancient civilization...the O-Parts.

In that world, a monster that strikes fear into the hearts of the strongest of men is rumored to exist. Those who have seen the monster all tell of the same thing—that the number of the beast, 666, is engraved on its forehead.

***

Jio, an O.P.T. boy who wants to rule the world, is traversing the globe with Ruby, a girl in search of both a legendary O-Part and her missing father. They reach Entotsu City, which suffers under the heel of government oppression, and are separated as they become entangled in an evil scheme. Jio teams up with Ball, a boy from the resistance movement, to defeat Jaga, Entotsu's wicked governor. But Jaga has now activated the terrifying O-Part Mexis – and Jio and Ball must also deal with Wise Yury, the Crimson Magician!!

Table of Contents

CHAPTER 18:

MARCHING ALONG THE WINDING ROAD

THE COWARD STRIKES BACK.

G G

O-PART: SHIN
RANK: SS

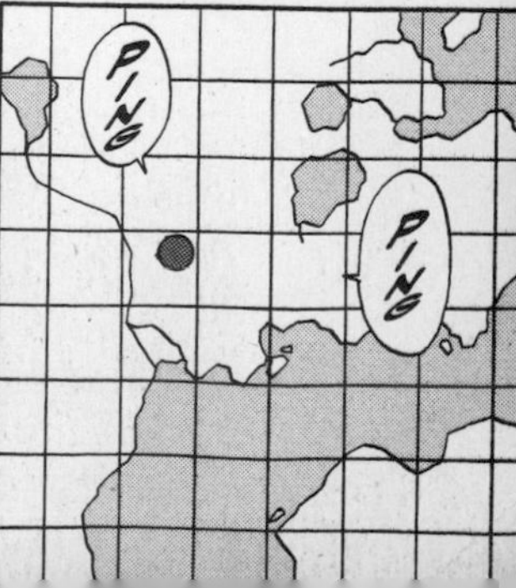

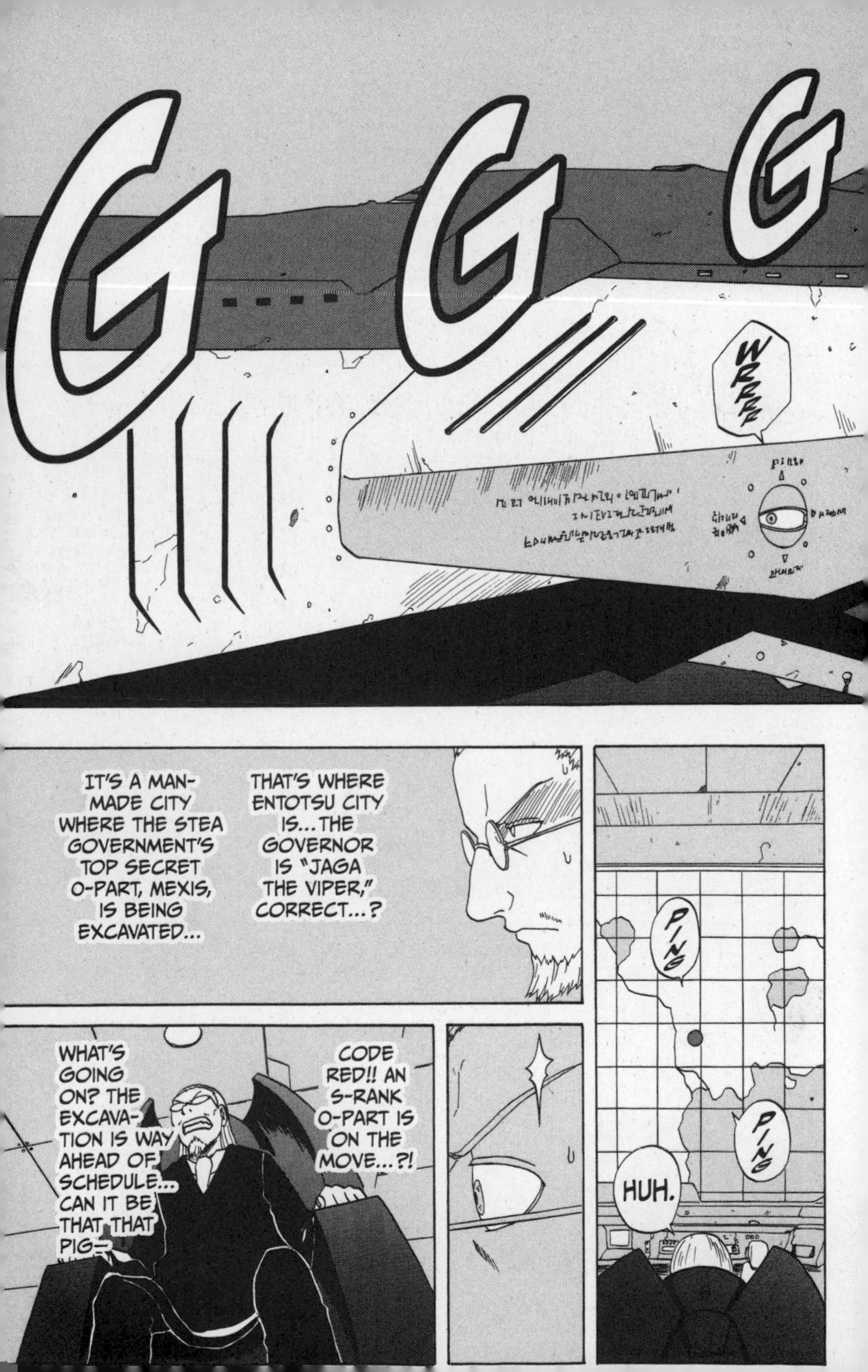

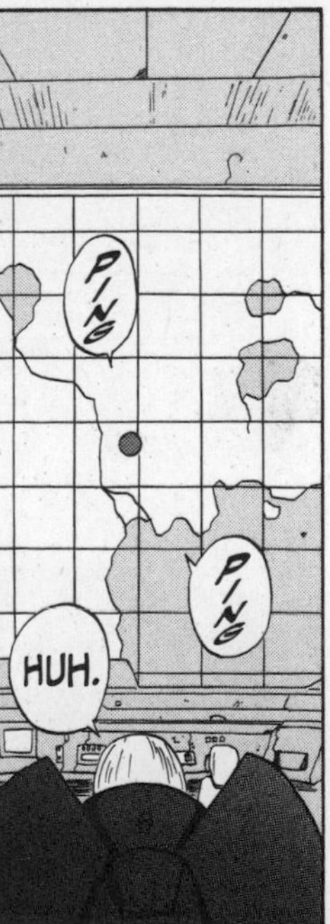

THAT'S WHERE ENTOTSU CITY IS...THE GOVERNOR IS "JAGA THE VIPER," CORRECT...?

IT'S A MAN-MADE CITY WHERE THE STEA GOVERNMENT'S TOP SECRET O-PART, MEXIS, IS BEING EXCAVATED...

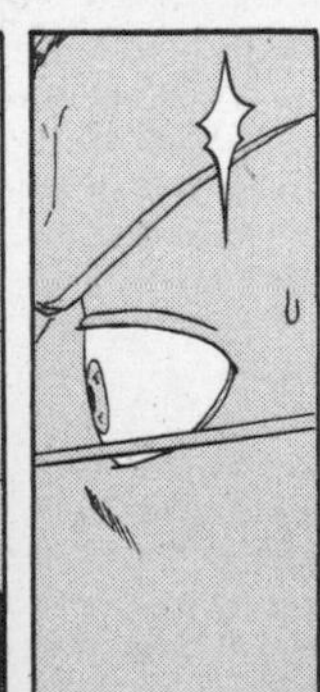

PLIP

WH... WHY WON'T MY SPIRIT COME OUT?!

YOU BRAT... HOW DARE YOU LOOK DOWN UPON ME LIKE SOME FOUR-LEGGED BEAST... JUST FOR THAT, I THINK I'LL TOY AROUND WITH YOU A LITTLE BIT...
HSSSH

HSSSH
...AND THEN SLICE YOU TO RIBBONS!!
JUST WATCH...
BM
INITIATE... EFFECT...

HEY, YOU'RE THE ONE WHO'S ON ALL FOURS!!
GWOOO
GWOOO
SWSH
WPSH
BIG BROTHER!!!
BALL!!!
HEH
PLIP
PLIP

AH... AAAH ...

I'M NOT GOING TO KILL YOU YET. LIKE I SAID, I'M GOING TO TOY AROUND WITH YOU FIRST.
SHHHHHH

CRCH

DM
DM
RUN FOR YOUR LIVES, EVERY-BODY!!!

WAIT FOR ME... WAIT... YOU HAVE TO PLAY WITH ME FIRST...
CLANK
CLANK

AAAARGH, JIO... HELP ME...

HUFF
HUFF

TP TP TP
HUFF
TP
TP
HUFF

WAIT FOR ME...
SHFF
SHFF

H...HE GIVES ME THE CREEPS!!! YO, HURRY UP GUYS, HE'S CATCHING UP!!!
DM
HUFF
DM
HUFF
DM
HUFF

HUFF
HUFF

TRIP

MARI!!
I... I CAN'T RUN ANY-MORE.
HUFF
HUFF
MARI !!!

HUFF
S...STOP JOKING! YO, THAT'S NOT SOMEBODY WE CAN DO ANYTHING AGAINST! WE'VE GOTTA RUN!!!
IF WE'RE GOING TO DIE, WE MIGHT AS WELL DIE FIGHTING! WE'RE MEMBERS OF THE RESISTANCE MOVEMENT TOO, YOU KNOW!!!
HUFF

O... OKAY.
CLINK
DAMN IT, IT'S NO USE TRYING TO RUN AWAY! WE'RE GOING TO HAVE TO DEFEAT HIM!!!
KLAK

AAARGH, HE'S CAUGHT UP WITH US.
I'M NOT GONNA FIGHT, YOU GUYS.

66LS
!!
CLANG

TP TP TP TP

B... BALL, ARE YOU RUNNING AWAY AGAIN?
HSSSH
COME ON, WE'RE READY TO FIGHT!!!

BIG BROTHER ...

DAMN IT, WHY AM I ALWAYS...

I DON'T CARE WHAT'S GONNA HAPPEN TO THEM!!!
DM
I'M ONLY A KID— I CAN'T FIGHT AGAINST AN O.P.T.!!!!
DM
DM

I... I...

JIO.
GRP

I'M GOING TO FULFILL MY DREAM, WHAT-EVER IT TAKES.
THAT'S WHY I'M WALKING ALONG THIS WINDING ROAD.

NCH
EVERY-BODY.

HUFF
HUFF
HUFF
HUFF

WIP

DAMN IT. OKAY, I'M NOT GONNA RUN AWAY.
BM
THIS AIN'T NO MAKE BELIEVE! I'M A REAL O.P.T.!!!!
NO MATTER HOW TOUGH THIS WINDING ROAD MAY BE... I'M GOING TO MARCH ALONG IT!!!

URGH.
NOW *I'M* THE ONE LOOKING DOWN *ON YOU.*
HOW DOES IT FEEL, HUH?

BM

B... BUT...
CLAP
MARI, RUN AWAY WHILE YOU STILL CAN!!!
AARGH.
HA HA...

THUD
YEE-ARGH!!!

BIG BROTHER!
BALL!

HUFF
HUFF

FUNNY JOKE, KID... YOU JUST WAIT AND SEE... I'M GOING TO KILL ALL OF YOU...STARTING WITH THE WEAKEST ONE...
KWP

Y... YO, YOU CAN RUN IF YOU WANT TO. I'M WILLING TO LET YOU GO.
WBBL
I...I HAPPEN TO BE AN O.P.T., YOU KNOW.
HUFF
HUFF
WBBL

YOUR BLUFF ISN'T GOING TO WORK AT A TIME LIKE THIS, BIG BROTHER.
YO, WAIT A MINUTE.
AND WHAT'S WITH USING THAT SAME OLD DUMB JOKE?

I JUST SAID THAT I'M AN O.P.T.—I'M THE ONE YOU'RE GONNA BE FIGHTING.
SO DON'T YOU DARE LAY A FINGER ON THE OTHERS!!
WBBL
BRRR
BRRR

LITTLE FOOL, YOU'RE SHAKING ALL OVER. DO YOU REALLY THINK I'M GOING TO BELIEVE THAT?
SHAK
SHAK
YOU'RE ALL GOING TO DIE!!
O.P.T.: MUSESHI
O-PART: HANG
O-PART RANK: C
EFFECT: ALTERATION OF PHYSICAL MATTER

HURRAY!

YEAH!

I DON'T CARE ABOUT WHAT'LL HAPPEN TO ME. I JUST WANT TO HELP THE OTHERS.

COME OUT, SPIRIT...

GRP

THEY'RE NOT JUST MY FRIENDS. US KIDS HAVE BEEN HELPING EACH OTHER OUT FOR A LONG TIME.

WE'RE A FAMILY!!!

HUH...
THAT'S...

I FINALLY UNDER-STAND...
...WHAT KIRIN MEANT.
SPIRIT IS A LIFE FORCE. IT'S A TYPE OF ENERGY THAT ONLY WORKS WHEN YOU THINK ABOUT SHARING IT WITH OTHERS INSTEAD OF USING IT FOR SELF-CENTERED REASONS. REMEMBER THAT.

BIG BROTHER, YOU REALLY...
SO YOU REALLY *DID* MEET KIRIN...
G G G G G G
WH...WHY IS THERE SPIRIT RISING OUT OF BALL'S BODY?!

I DON'T KNOW WHAT'S HAPPENED TO HIM, BUT HE REALLY HAS BECOME AN O.P.T.!!!!
HA HA, IT'S REALLY NOT A DREAM.
THAT'S AWESOME, BALL.

BALL, YOU...
BWA

TCH...I NEVER THOUGHT THAT THIS BRAT WAS A REAL O.P.T....

THD

BIG BROTHER.

TUG

GHP

INITIATE EFFECT!!!
VOOOOO

HUH.

FWP
KP

PAP

ANY SUSPICIOUS PUNKS GET A TASTE OF MY O-PART, AND IT'S GONNA BE INSTANT DEATH FOR THEM.

YO, YOU BETTER START MAKING FUNERAL ARRANGE-MENTS, 'CUZ YOU'VE GOT A FIGHT COMIN'.

O.P.T.: BALL
O-PART: COOL BALL (PICKLE STONE)
O-PART RANK: C
EFFECT: MAGNET (MAGNETISM)

LET'S RAISE THE VOLUME!!!

ZM

HUH.

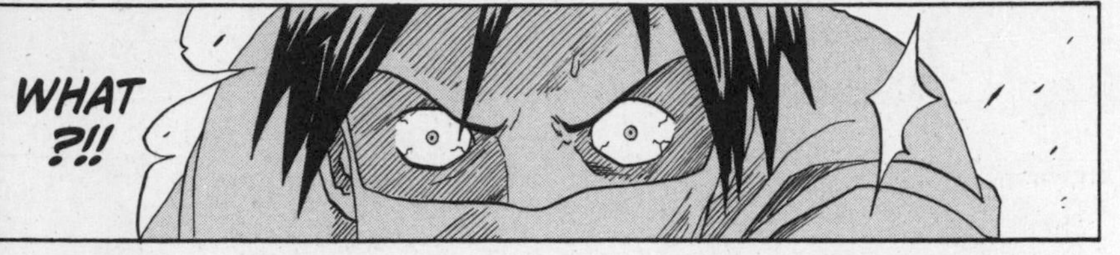

GSH GSH

WHAT WAS THAT ABOUT YOU PIERCING SOMETHING?

Sp Sp Sp Sp

BSHOOOOO
TAKE THIS—MAGNET ATTACK!!!

SO THIS IS WHAT A BATTLE BETWEEN O.P.T.S IS LIKE... W... WOW...

WOW, BALL!!!

IT'S FAST!!!

KRCH
DOOOSH
ZSH
AAAH, HE DODGED IT!!!
DAMN IT.
I...I MISSED.
CLAK
GRA AAA
PSH
CLAK
CLAK
THAT WAS CLOSE...THAT WAS CLOSE... IT WAS FASTER THAN I THOUGHT IT WOULD BE...
BUT...THIS TIME, YOU'VE GOT NOTHING TO PROTECT YOUR-SELF WITH...
NOW WHAT ARE YOU GOING TO DO?!!

RUN, BALL!!!
BIG BROTHER!!
MAGNET, NEGATIVE POLE!!!
BM
BOOF
WHAT?!
SWSH
GRA
AA

UUUURGH!

HURRAY!

HA HA, HOW DID YOU LIKE THAT MAGNETIC ENEMA?!

OWW... MY ASS...
MY ASS... MY ASS...
WUBB

OH.

SNAP
AAAAAAAARGH!
I'M STANDING ...!!!

IT'S SO HIGH UP HERE...! I'M SCARED...!! THE GROUND'S SO FAR DOWN!!!

?!!
...

SO HE'S GOT AN EXTREME CASE OF ACROPHO-BIA?!!
WHA... WHAT'S WRONG WITH THE GUY?!

GROUND, GROUND!! SAFE AND SECURE!!!
HUFF
CLAK
HUFF

HUFF
PANT
HUFF
PANT
NOW YOU'VE REALLY MADE ME ANGRY!
EH, SERIOUSLY, I...
...ONLY MADE YOU STAND UP BY HITTING YOU IN THE BUTTOCKS.
MAXIMUM SPIRIT! NOW IT'S MY TURN TO HAVE YOU STAND UP!!!
GWOOO
SLASH
DAMN.
DM
GOSH

GRRCH

HUH... SO YOU'VE USED THAT STONE TO MOVE MY CLAW OUT OF THE WAY.
BUT...

TINKK
PLIP
PLIP
WHOA!

WHOA, THE CLAW CHANGED ITS DIRECTION AND BEGAN TO STRETCH EVEN LONGER!!!
BE CAREFUL, BALL!!!
DM DM DM
AAAAH... YO, THIS AIN'T FAIR!!!
SWSH SWSH

DMP
SWSH
WHOA.

OH NO!!!

BIG BROTHER!!!

SP
?!

TCH.
HUH.
I ALMOST HAD YOU, BUT MY CLAW'S AT ITS LIMIT.

BUT IN ORDER TO DO THAT, I'M GOING TO HAVE TO TRY AND STRETCH THE CLAW OUT AS LONG AS I CAN, DODGE IT AS IT COMES AT ME AND IMMEDIATELY ATTACK HIM.

CALM DOWN... GOTTA REMEMBER ALL THE TRAINING I'VE DONE AT KIRIN'S PLACE. THERE MUST BE SOMETHING I CAN DO...

TPTPTPTP
HUH.

THAT'S RIGHT, JAJA-MARU!! I'M GOING TO GIVE IT A SHOT...

!!

OKAY.
PT

BALL.
HE'S GOING TO RUN AWAY AFTER ALL!!

HA HA HA, SO, YOU'RE GOING TO RUN AWAY, YOU COWARD!!

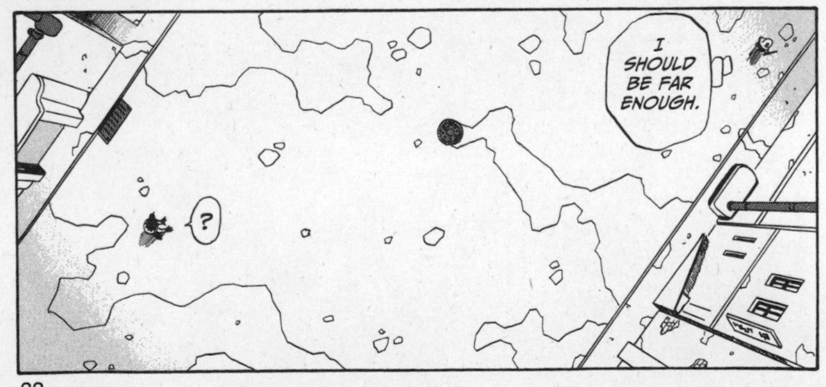
I SHOULD BE FAR ENOUGH.
?

WHA... WHAT?
TP
WHA... WHAT IS HE UP TO?
WHAT ARE YOU MAKING HIM EVEN ANGRIER FOR?
SHAKK
I'VE HAD IT WITH YOU LOOKING DOWN ON ME. DIE!!!
TAKE THIS!!
SHAKK
DOUBLE HANG RUN!!!
GOOD, HE FELL FOR IT.
DM

ZWSH
DAMN, WHY'S BALL RUNNING OVER TO MUSESHI?!
HE'S GONNA GET KILLED!!!
SWSH
TP
LOOK HOW FAR HE'S JUMPED! I CAN'T BELIEVE THAT THAT'S REALLY BALL!!!
BUT HE'S JUMPED TOO FAST TO DODGE THE CLAWS. LOOK!
GOTCHA. THE GROUND'S THE SAFEST PLACE TO BE. YOU'RE NOTHING BUT A TARGET UP IN THE AIR, ESPECIALLY SINCE IT'S IMPOSSIBLE FOR YOU TO CHANGE DIRECTIONS.
SWSH
BND

WHIZZZZZ
HEH.
TMP
SWISH

TAKE THIS!
YEAH, I DID IT. A SUC-CESSFUL COUNTER ATTACK.
FLIP
WHAT?!! HE KICKED OFF FROM THE STONE!!!
D... DAMN IT. I'VE CHANGED THE CLAW'S DIRECTION...
...BUT I CAN'T STRETCH IT ANY MORE. I DON'T HAVE TIME TO PULL IT BACK, EITHER.
KNN
KNN
RRSSH
OK!!!
YEAH, BALL! GO FOR IT!!!

GRRRT
!!!
HA HA, YOU WERE DOING PRETTY WELL UNTIL A MOMENT AGO.
WHAT'S WITH YOUR MOUTH ?!!
I CHANGED MY TEETH INTO O-PARTS AS WELL.
GRRT
AND I CAN DISLOCATE MY JAW TO EAT YOU.
GRRT
SP SP SP SP
SHOOT, THE CLAWS ARE COMING BACK.

I CAN KILL YOU WITH JUST MY MOUTH!!!
SHA
CREK
VOO
SHAK
AAAAAAH!
CRUNCH
SWSHHH
AAA-ARGH ...!!
HA HA, THESE TEETH ARE SLOWLY GOING TO BITE INTO YOU.
BIG BROTHER!
COME ON, LET'S HELP BALL!!

IF YOU'RE GOING TO PULL IT BACK, ONCE IT COMES NEAR YOU, YOU'VE GOT TO SWITCH TO THE SAME POLES AND LOWER THE O-PART'S SPEED— OR YOU'LL DIE.

NO, YOU SERIOUSLY AREN'T GOING TO...?!!
GRRRGH
!!
YOU'RE TRYING TO KILL YOUR-SELF ALONG WITH ME!! G...GET OFF, LET ME GO!
FWAP
FWAP
BIG BROTHER!!
BALL !!!

OOOSH

FSH
FSH

FSH
SP

SHHHH

HA HA HA HA HA, THAT STUPID BRAT. HE MISSED ME AND KILLED HIMSELF...

BAK

HUH?

THIS IS WHAT I MEANT.

PHEEEEEEEEUUUW
PSSS

...ME ...
GLUG GLUG

HELP ...

TMP
THUD

WBBL
I WANTED TO RUN AWAY... I WAS SO SCARED... SERIOUSLY ...

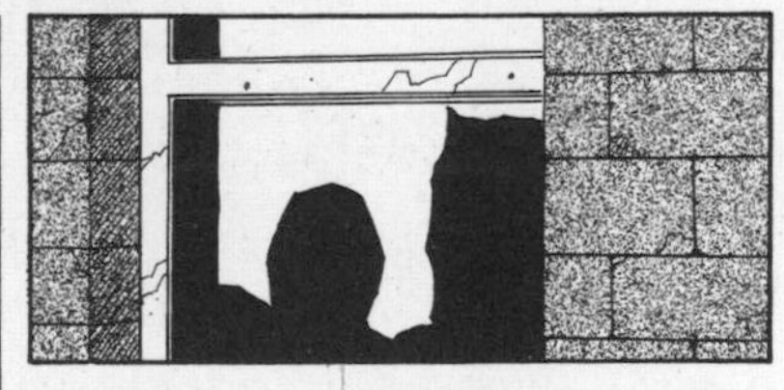

THUD
BUT I WON...
YO...

I CAN'T BELIEVE A KID THAT YOUNG IS FIGHTING AGAINST ZENOM...
AND THE ADULTS ARE JUST RUNNING AROUND.

HEY, BALL, HANG IN THERE! HEY!!!
BIG BROTHER!
BALL!

THEY'RE ALL CRYING.

PLIP
PLIP
IT'S SO WARM ...

YES, HE'S REGAINED CONSCIOUS-NESS. ARE YOU OKAY, BALL?!
YO, ARE YOU GUYS OKAY? YOU'RE ALL CRYING.
STOP IT, BIG BROTHER.
JIO... WENT STRAIGHT ALONG THE WINDING ROAD TOO.

SCURCH

HUH...

SCURCH

CRRR
THE TV TURNED ON!!
LOOKS LIKE THE LEADER SUCCEEDED IN GETTING INSIDE.

TRN
TRN
CREEEEE

TP

SO THIS IS THE GOVERNMENT'S BROADCAST STATION.
LUCK'S ON MY SIDE— NO ONE'S AROUND.

GREETINGS, MY FELLOW CITIZENS.
SCRCH

IT'S NOT THE LEADER!!!
DAMN IT, IT'S JAGA!!

HEY, ARE YOU FILMING ME PROPERLY?
I'M GLAD I BROUGHT THIS ALONG WITH THE SPIRIT DRIVES.
THE STEAM IS INTERFERING WITH THE TV SIGNALS...
...BUT IT SHOULD BE OKAY.

GOOD.

EH... STARTING FROM TODAY, I...

...AM NO LONGER THE GOVERNOR OF THIS CITY.

WHAT'S JAGA TALKING ABOUT?
I DUNNO. I HAVEN'T GOT A CLUE.

I HAVE BECOME A GOD.

NOT ONLY THIS TOWN, BUT THE CONTINENT OF ASCALD... NO, ALL THE CONTINENTS...

...NO, NO, NO, THE WHOLE WIDE WORLD IS MINE NOW. I'M A TRULY GREAT BEING.

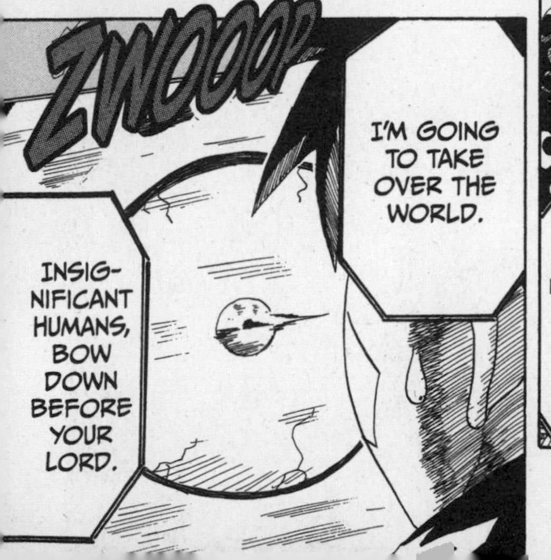

DAMN, AM I TOO LATE?!!

TCH.

OH, THIS IS SO GREAT! I'VE ALWAYS WANTED TO SAY THAT IN FRONT OF ALL THESE PESKY HUMANS!
YOU SEE, I'M A GOD!
IT'S, IT'S, IT'S, IT'S...
MUNCH
MUNCH

...ECSTASY ...

KWOOP

EH ?

WHA... WHAT IS THIS?!!
ZLOOOSH!

CHAPTER 19:
EVERYBODY'S THOUGHTS AND FEELINGS

AAAA-ARGH!!!

ZLLIP

WHAT IS THIS?!
ZWOOP

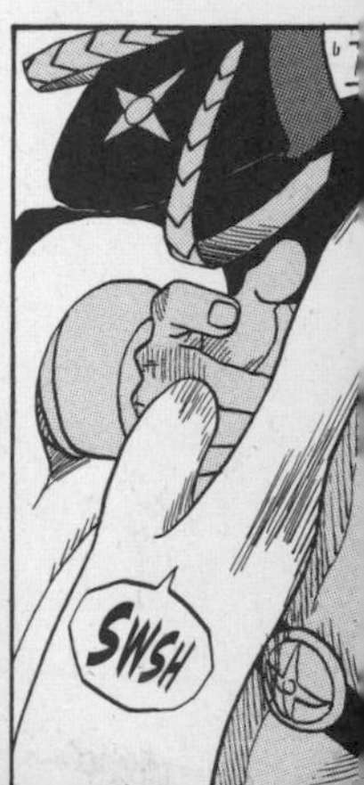
SWSH

!!

IT... IT'S DRAG-GING ME INSIDE!!
ZLLSH
GWUB GWUB

EEE-AARGH!

WHAT'S GOING ON?!
HURRY UP AND HELP ME!!

DMP
AH!

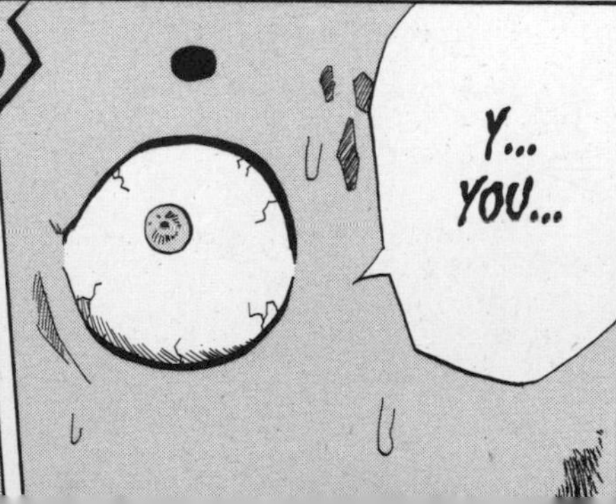
Y... YOU...

...

SP
WHA... WHAT? WHAT HAPPENED TO JAGA?
ZCRRCH
CRRCH
Y... YOU...
ZRRCH
WHERE IS THIS IMAGE BEING SENT FROM, AND WHAT'S HAPPENING OUT THERE?!

DAMN IT, WHATEVER'S GOING ON OUT THERE, I CAN'T LINK UP TO THE TV SCREENS IN TOWN FROM HERE.
DID THE GOVERN-MENT KNOW ABOUT OUR PLAN?

SO YOU'RE THE LEADER OF THE RESISTANCE MOVEMENT. IT'S JUST AS WISE SAID.
YOU CAME ALL THIS WAY JUST TO BE KILLED...
DOOM

TCH!! HOW DID YOU GET IN HERE?
BM
ZWP
OOPS.

HA HA... THAT MONSTER HAS ALREADY STARTED MOVING. IT'S IMPOSSIBLE TO STOP IT NOW.

STOP TRYING TO RESIST AND JUST BE LIKE THE OTHER PEOPLE IN THIS TOWN.
COM-PLETELY UNABLE TO DO ANY-THING...
BLOOP

DAMN.
...AND WALLOWING IN DESPAIR...

BM
SO, HURRY UP AND DIE LOOKING DOWN!!

CRASH
BM

!!

JIO!!

NUUR-
RGH!!!

SPNN
CRCH
WHAM
FSH
FSH
CLAK
CLAK

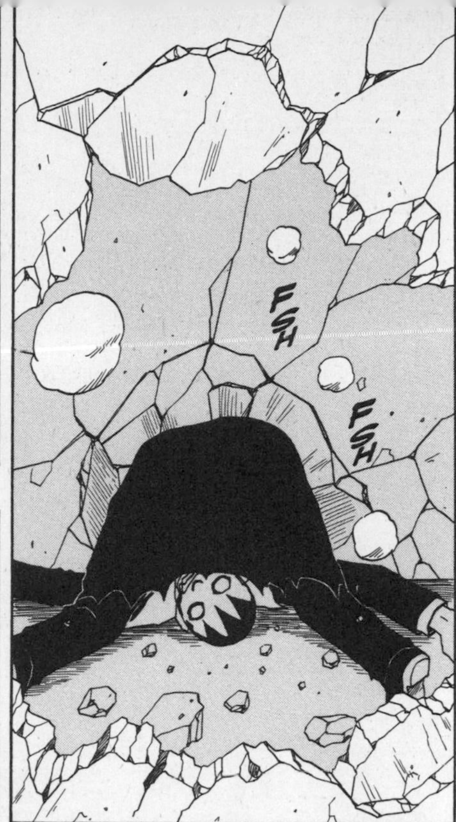
FSH
FSH

YOU GUYS ARE THE ONES GOING DOWN, ZENOM.

JIO!! WHAT ARE YOU DOING HERE?!

WHAT ARE *YOU* DOING HERE? ARE YOU SPYING ON THE GOVERNMENT?
I KEPT THE FINAL OPERATION A SECRET FROM ALL YOU KIDS...
...BUT IT LOOKS LIKE IT'S TOO LATE.

FINAL OPERATION?

THAT'S RIGHT. I WAS GOING TO PLAY THIS TAPE SO ALL THE CITIZENS COULD SEE IT ON TV AND FIND OUT THE TRUTH.
AFTER THAT, WE WERE GOING TO DESTROY ALL THE MAJOR STEAM PIPES, CUTTING OFF ALL THE POWER IN TOWN...

I CAME ALL THE WAY DOWN HERE BELIEVING THAT THE PEOPLE WOULD RETURN TO THE WAY THEY USED TO BE AND STOP BEING THE GOVERNMENT'S SLAVES ONCE THEY KNEW THE TRUTH, BUT...

...IT'S ALL USELESS NOW. I COULDN'T DO ANY-THING.
SWP
WE'RE ALL GOING TO DIE.

SNAP

WHAT'S... THE MEANING OF THIS, JIO...

CLAK

JIO...

THEN I'LL KILL YOU, LEADER.

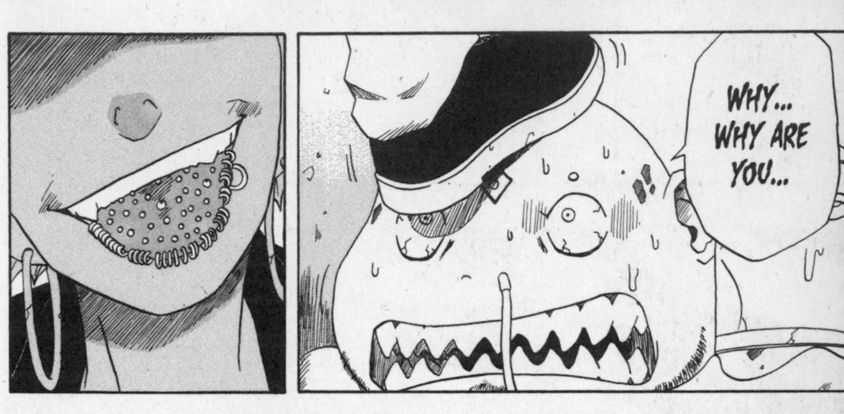

WISE !!!

HOW'S LIFE, MY DEAR GOVERNOR?

WHA...WHAT? DOC, HURRY UP AND DO SOMETHING ABOUT HIM!!
EH.

I'M SORRY, BUT I'M GOING TO HAVE TO ASK YOU TO DIE.
I THANK YOU FOR ALL YOU'VE DONE FOR ME.
GRSH GRSH

CLONK

TCH!!!
SWP

HUH.

GOOD!! USE THAT GUN AND KILL HIM!

HA... HA HA... DOC, W-WHAT KIND OF JOKE IS THIS?

YOU IDIOT. DID YOU SERIOUSLY THINK THAT THE ZENOM SYNDICATE WOULD JOIN HANDS WITH THE GOVERN-MENT?

THE SACRIFICE USED TO POWER MEXIS...

HSSSSH

...THAT'S WHAT YOU ARE, YOU DRUGGED-UP PIG.
HUH ?!!

MY REAL NAME IS BROWNY SCHRETZ, A SCIENTIST FROM THE ZENOM SYNDICATE.
YOU'VE PROBABLY HEARD OF ME BEFORE.

YOU'RE DR. BROWNY?! WHAT ARE YOU DOING WITH THE ZENOM SYNDICATE?!!

SIMPLE. THE SYNDICATE WAS THE ONLY PLACE THAT ACCEPTED MY RESEARCH.
THAT'S WHY I WAS ABLE TO COMPLETE THE SPIRIT DRIVE.
CHAK
DOOM

I MADE ADVANCEMENTS TOWARD THE GOVERNMENT AS A SPY FROM ZENOM AND CHOSE YOU, JAGA, AS MY GUINEA PIG TO DO MY EXPERIMENTS ON.
MY RESEARCH WAS ONLY ABOUT 80 PERCENT COMPLETE, BUT...

...I KEPT ADMINISTERING THE GOD'S MEDICINE R-108, WHICH I CREATED, AND FORCED YOUR BODY TO BECOME AN O.P.T.
PSH

THE MEDICINE'S SIDE-EFFECTS WILL DESTROY THE FRONTAL LOBE OF YOUR BRAIN, MAKING YOU GO CRAZY. ALSO, YOU WILL SOON EXPERIENCE EXCRUCIATING PAIN IN YOUR INTERNAL ORGANS.
YOU'VE ONLY GOT ABOUT A MONTH LEFT TO LIVE, ANYWAY.
HEH
SO WHY DON'T YOU MAKE YOUR DEATH A USEFUL ONE?

ONE.
TWO.
THREE.
FOUR.
AND JAGA...

YOU'RE THE FIFTH SPIRIT DRIVE!!

HOW DARE YOU DECEIVE ME!!
HA HA HA HA, YOU STILL INSIST ON CALLING YOURSELF A GOD, HUH?
TALK ABOUT A FALL FROM GRACE.

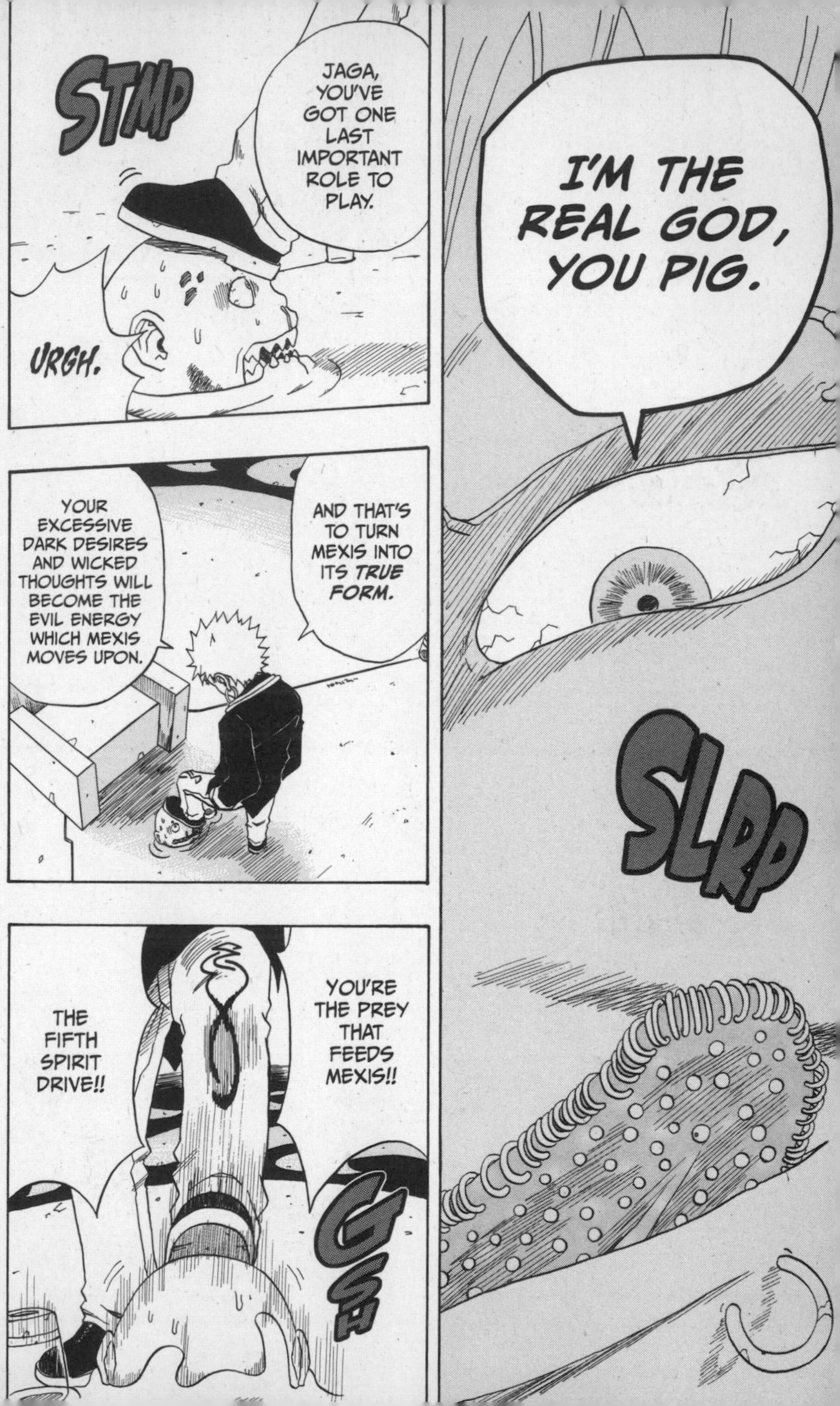

I'M THE REAL GOD, YOU PIG.

SLRP

ZZZLLSH
NO, THIS WASN'T HOW THINGS WERE SUPPOSED TO TURN OUT!

HELP!!
HELP ME!!

ZLLLSSH
GO...
...D ...

SHWP ...

TP

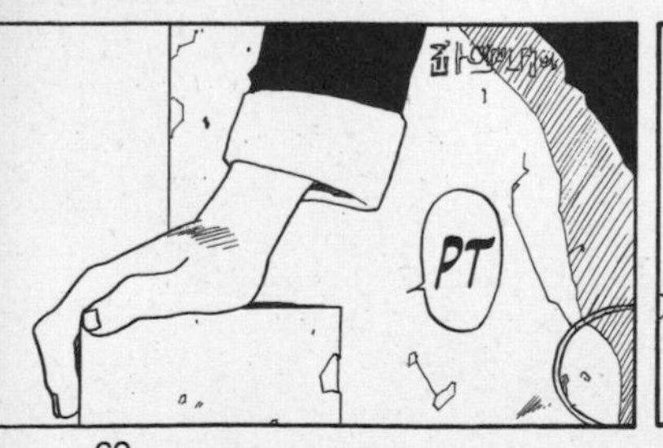
PT

DOOOM

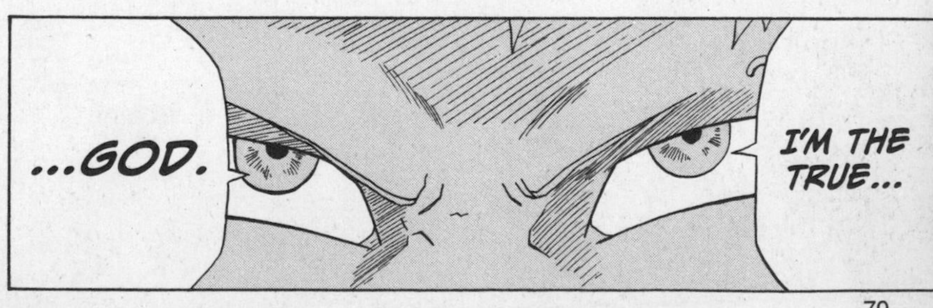

HSSSH
BZAP
BZAP

IT'S TIME FOR YOU TO SHOW YOUR TRUE FORM, TOO.

IT'S BEGUN TO TRANS-FORM!!

SQUSSSH

BM
FWAP
FWAP
BZAP
ZLSH

CRRSH

CREK CREK

BZAP

SQSH

HSSSSH

CREK

FWIP
FWIP
SQUSSH

TH...THAT MONSTER IS CHANGING SHAPE.
HUFF
HUFF
HUFF

IT'S OVER. WE'RE FINISHED— AND SO IS THE TOWN.

THEY USED US TO EXCAVATE THAT *THING*, AND NOW WE'RE GOING TO BE KILLED BECAUSE THEY NO LONGER NEED US.

LOOK, AMIDABA, THAT MONSTER'S TRANS-FORMING.
WHAT IN THE WORLD IS GOING ON?

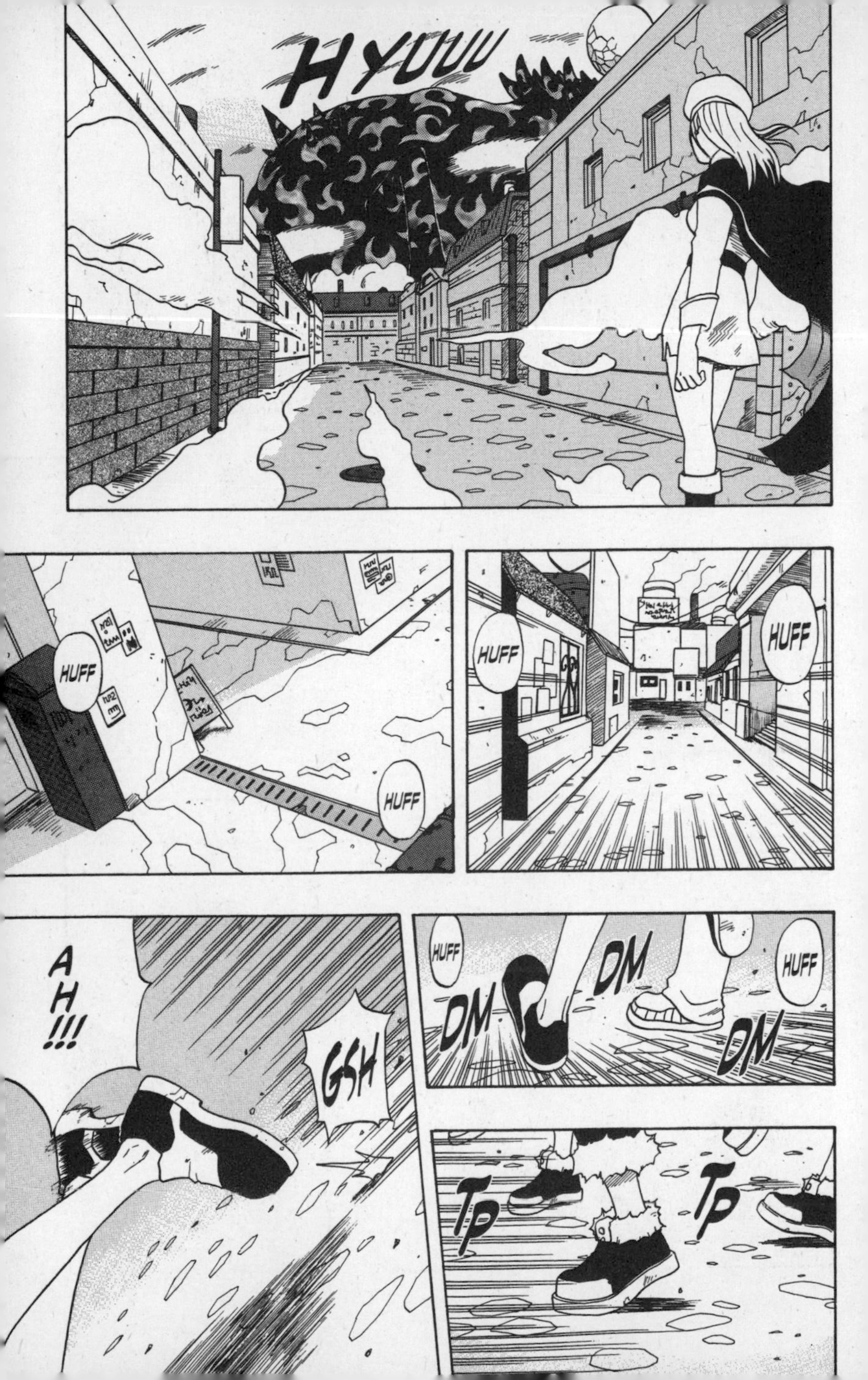

HYUUU

ARE YOU OKAY, SPHERE?!

HUFF

I THINK I'VE SPRAINED MY LEG.

HUFF

YOU GO AHEAD ON YOUR OWN.

HUFF
HUFF
DM
WHAT'S THE MATTER?! ARE YOU OKAY?
DON'T COME NEAR US!!
WE DON'T NEED ANY HELP FROM YOU GOVERNMENT THUGS.
HUH?!
OH, WELL, THIS IS...
CRCH
HUFF
HUFF

HEY, WE'VE FOUND TWO MORE RATS...

DOOM

FOUR RATS ALTOGETHER. WHICH ONE SHALL WE KILL FIRST?

AMIDABA!! DID YOU HEAR THAT? WHAT ARE WE GOING TO DO?
DO SOME-THING!
I... I CAN'T.
I'VE USED UP ALL MY SPIRIT COMING HERE.

NO WAY!

CHAK
LET'S DO IT.
HURRAY.
CHAK

B
M
AAAAH!

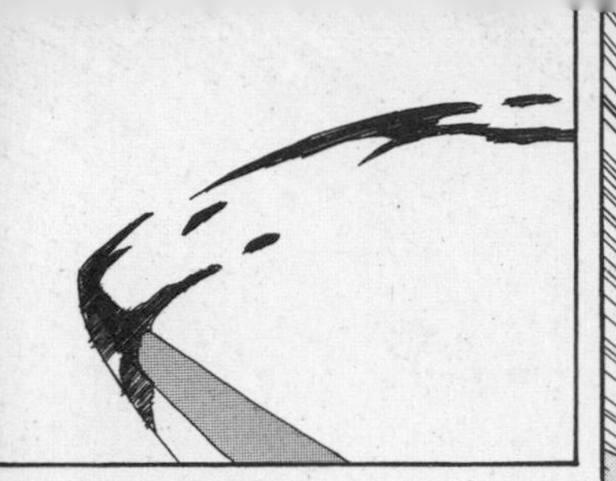

HUH.

WHAT?!

YOU'RE—!!
!!

SP

SSHP

I KNEW IT.

THUD

CITY LIFE DOESN'T SUIT ME.

CLIK

POOF
URGH!!!

KWP

HE... HE'S TOO FAST. WHO IS HE...?

SWP
THD
...
ONCE YOU DRAW YOUR SWORD, YOU'RE PUTTING YOUR LIFE ON THE LINE. NEVER FORGET THAT.

AMIDABA!!!
WHAT?

IT REALLY IS YOU.
KIRIN.

THIS TOWN IS SO ROWDY NO MATTER WHEN I COME.

HUH, YOU KNOW THIS DODGY LOOKING GUY, AMIDABA?
THAT'S NOT ALL.
RUBY, THIS IS THE MAN WHO APPRAISED THAT PENDANT OF YOURS.
HE WAS ALSO A MEMBER OF THE STEA ARMY'S SPECIAL FORCES.
DODGY LOOKING GUY
OH, THEN HE WAS WITH MY FATHER...

NO, KIRIN'S NOT AN O.P.T. HE WAS THE ONLY PERSON IN THE SPECIAL FORCES...
...WHO WAS A COMPLETELY NORMAL HUMAN.
HUH... BUT THAT'S...
HE'S A GENIUS, YOU SEE.
I'VE NEVER BEEN TOO FOND OF AMIDABA.
?

A GENIUS ...
KIRIN IS...
GGGG
AH!
!

THUD

VREEEE
THE SYNDICATE'S PLAN IS ABSOLUTE. AND WE NOW HAVE MEXIS IN OUR HANDS.
WE'VE GOT NO USE FOR THIS CITY NOW.

WHAT'S GOING ON?!!
FCCCH

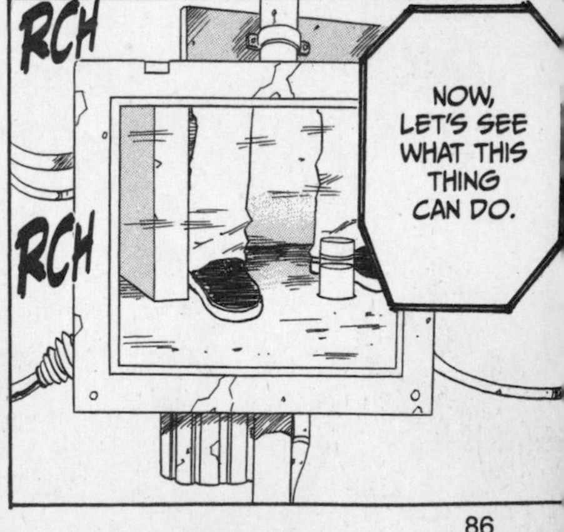
NOW, LET'S SEE WHAT THIS THING CAN DO.
RCH
RCH

DAMN IT, THAT VOICE AND THOSE SHOES. IT'S WISE, ALL RIGHT.

IF YOU'RE GOING TO DIE, IT DOESN'T MAKE A DIFFERENCE WHO KILLS YOU, RIGHT?
BUT I'D RATHER DIE FIGHTING.

DMP

DAMN, I KNEW IT! WISE IS ON THE TOP OF THAT MONSTER!!

DM DM DM
JIO!! WHERE DO YOU THINK YOU'RE GOING?!!

WHERE ELSE?
TO WHERE WISE IS!!
DP

YOU'RE GOING TO FIGHT THAT O-PART?!! THAT'S IMPOSSI-BLE!!!
EVEN THOUGH YOU'RE AN O.P.T., YOU'RE NO MATCH FOR THAT THING. THE RESULT WAS OBVIOUS FROM THE START!!

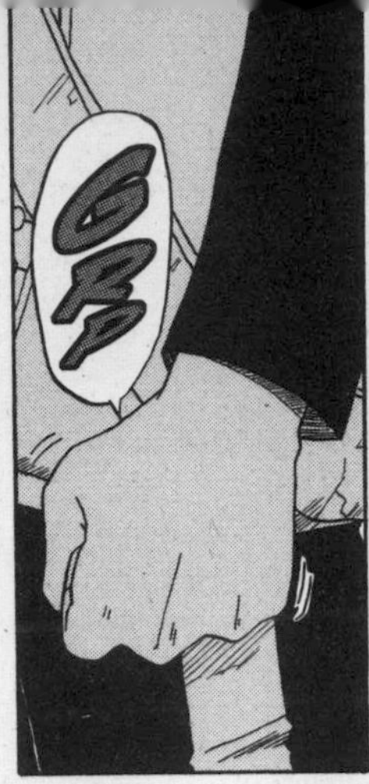
GRP

I'VE ALREADY TOLD YOU, LEADER, THAT I'VE GOT A DREAM...
...AND I'VE GOT NO TIME TO WASTE IN A PLACE LIKE THIS...

BUT YOU MIGHT DIE.
THE PEOPLE OF THIS TOWN ARE JUST LIKE THE WAY I USED TO BE.

THE PEOPLE OF ENTOTSU CITY ARE JUST LIKE THE WAY YOU...
...USED TO BE?

...THAT YOU CAN'T CHANGE ANYTHING, AND THAT NOTHING'S GOING TO CHANGE, *IF YOU KEEP CRYING AND RUNNING AWAY.*

...SHE'S AN IMPOR-TANT...

...FRIEND OF MINE.

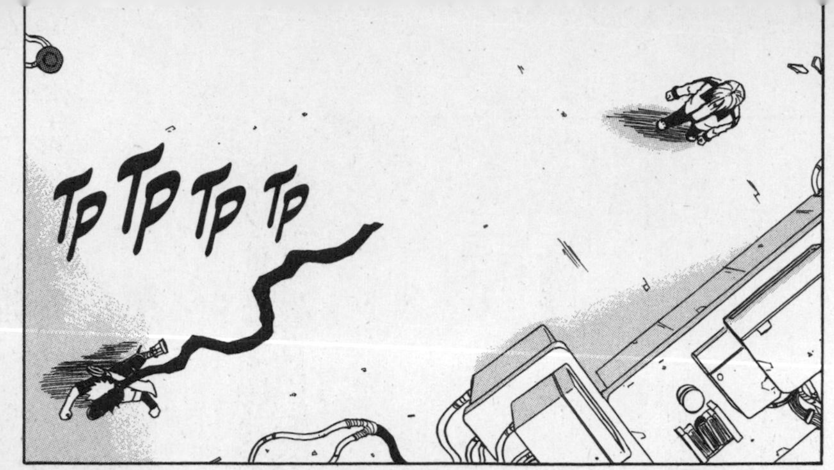
Tp Tp Tp Tp

JIO!!!

Z
M

WHAT IS THIS DREAM OF YOURS?

WHAT NOW?
OOOH, JUST LET ME GO. IT WOULD HAVE LOOKED SO COOL IF YOU HADN'T STOPPED ME.

WORLD DOMINA-
TION.

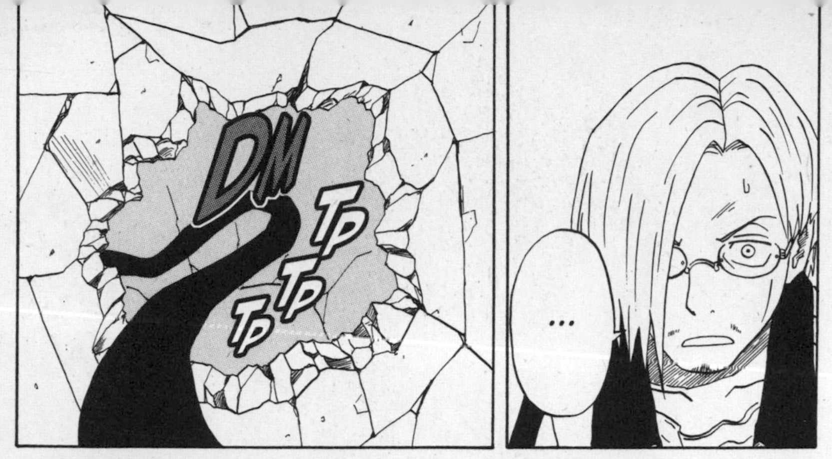
DM
TP TP TP
...

HE'S RIGHT— WHAT AM I DOING? IT'S STILL TOO EARLY TO GIVE UP!
THERE MUST BE SOME-THING I CAN DO!

G G G G G G G

SNIFF
SNIFF

FASH
ZWSH
IT'S LIKE LOOKING AT THE SUN.
A... AMAZING.

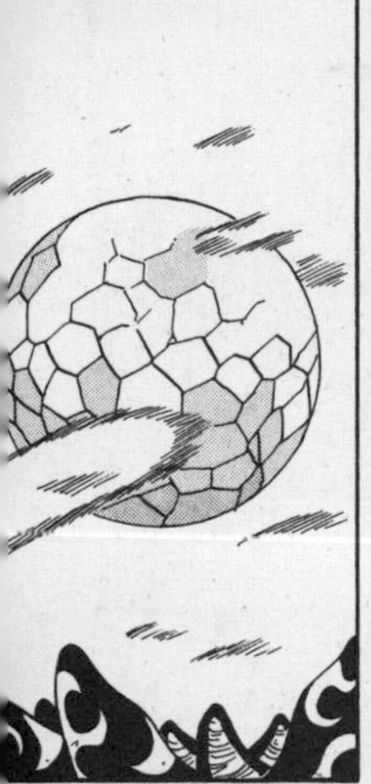

DM DM

SHHH

SHA
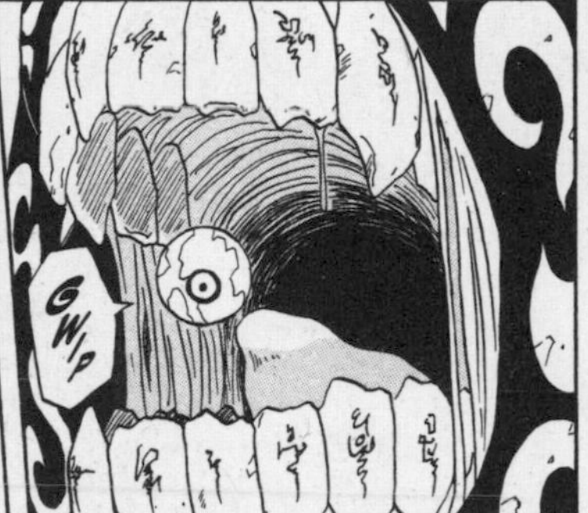
GWIP

DM DM

HUH, HE STILL HASN'T GIVEN UP YET.

ZM

CHAPTER 20:
FINAL OPERATION

REMEMBER, YOU'RE *MY* PLAYTHING. IT'S TIME TO HAVE SOME FUN.

VEEEN

HUH ?!
WHAT'S THAT?!

RSSHHH

OOOPS, DIDN'T MEAN TO OVERDO IT...
MAYBE I KILLED HIM...
SHHHHH

URGH.

WHA...WHAT WAS THAT? SOME KIND OF LASER BEAM?!!
HUFF
HOW AM I SUPPOSED TO GET CLOSE UP?

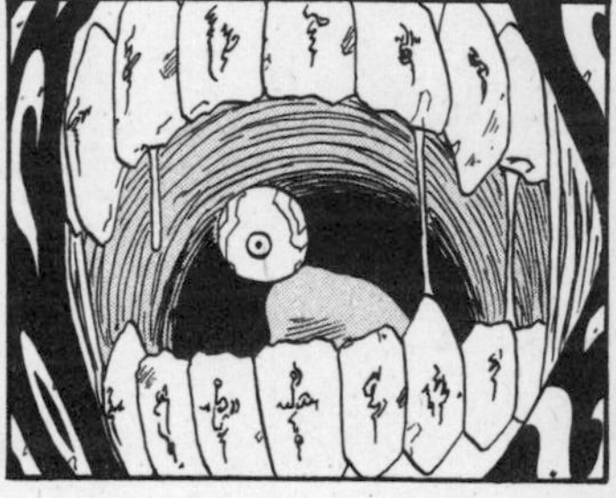

HEY, HE'S ALIVE, HE'S ALIVE! GOOD, GOOD, THAT'S GREAT!

IF THAT THING HITS ME, I'LL BE TURNED INTO A PILE OF DUST.
DAMN... WHAT AM I SUPPOSED TO DO?

HSSS

YO, WHAT'S WITH THAT? YOU SOUND LIKE YOU'RE UNHAPPY TO SEE ME.

FORGET IT. DO YOU HAVE ANY IDEA WHERE YOU ARE?

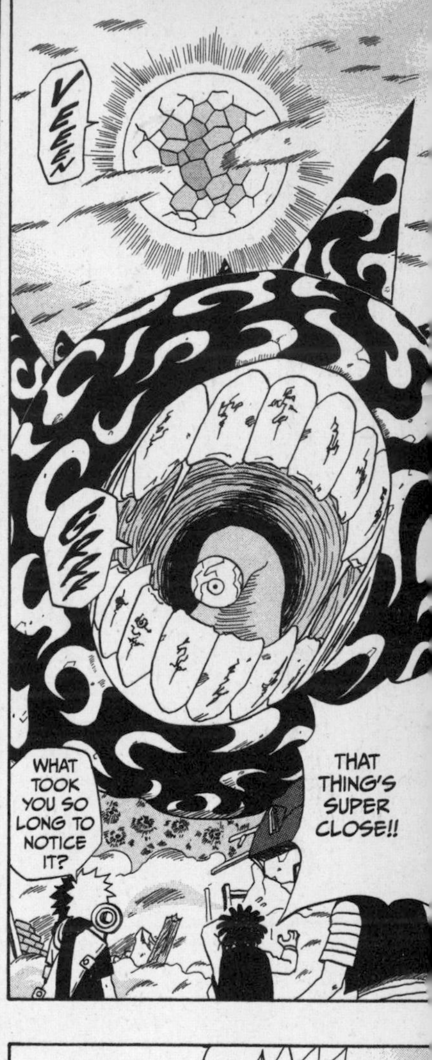
VEEEN
THAT THING'S SUPER CLOSE!!
WHAT TOOK YOU SO LONG TO NOTICE IT?

I REMEMBER YOU TWO. YOU'RE THOSE NO-GOOD PUNKS FROM THE RESISTANCE MOVEMENT.

DON'T YOU MAKE FUN OF THE RESISTANCE MOVEMENT, DAMN IT! I'M NOT GONNA RUN AWAY ANYMORE! EVERYBODY'S DOING ALL THEY CAN!

EVERYBODY IN THE RESISTANCE MOVEMENT...

I WAS GOING TO PLAY THIS TAPE SO ALL THE CITIZENS COULD SEE IT ON TV AND FIND OUT THE TRUTH.
AFTER THAT, WE WERE GOING TO DESTROY ALL THE MAJOR STEAM PIPES, CUTTING OFF ALL THE POWER IN TOWN...

AAAH, I'VE GOT NO TIME TO THINK ABOUT IT! THERE'S NO OTHER CHOICE!!

IF I CAN FIND A WAY TO CONTACT THE LEADER, THEN HE CAN COMMUNICATE WITH THE RESISTANCE MEMBERS THROUGH THE TV SCREENS IN TOWN...

JIO!!

AAAAH!

ZOOM!!

BALL!!

CONTACT THE LEADER UP IN THE GOVERNMENT'S BROADCAST ROOM AND TELL HIM TO COMMENCE THE FINAL OPERATION.

FINAL OPERA-TION?

WHOA.

HSSS

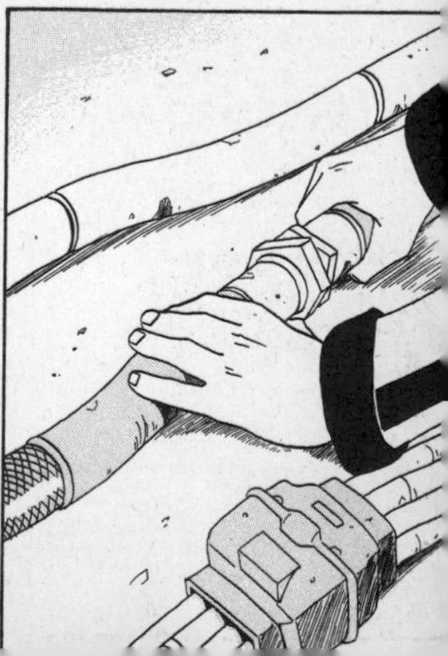

RRRR

...

CLICK

WHO IS IT?

HEY, YO, LEADER. WOW, IT'S JUST AS JIO SAID.
BINGO!!
BALL!! YOU'RE SAFE?!

I GOT CHESS TO FIND OUT THE PHONE NUMBER OF THE PLACE YOU'RE AT.
EVERY-BODY'S DOING FINE.
IF IT'S SOME-THING LIKE THIS, LEAVE IT TO ME.
TEL
PIP

LEADER, LEADER, GUESS WHAT? I ACTUALLY DEFEATED AN O.P.T. FROM ZENOM!!

BALL, STOP JOKING AROUND.
SO, DID YOU MEET UP WITH JIO?! WHAT'S THE MATTER?!

WHAT'S WRONG? HEY, ANSWER ME.
Ughn
I GUESS IT'S TOO HARD FOR HIM TO BELIEVE THAT BALL ACTUALLY...

I'M NOT SURE WHAT HE MEANT, BUT JIO TOLD ME TO TELL YOU TO COMMENCE THE FINAL OPERATION!!

WHAT ?!
JIO.

AND A WHILE AGO, SHE TOLD ME THAT YOU CAN'T CHANGE ANYTHING, AND THAT NOTHING'S GOING TO CHANGE...
...IF YOU KEEP CRYING AND RUNNING AWAY...

JIO, I'M GOING TO BELIEVE YOU. IF YOU'RE TELLING ME TO DO IT, I'LL DO IT.
AND I'LL PASS ON HOW YOU FEEL TO EVERY-BODY!!

RRKSS

WHAT'S GOING ON?
THE TOWN... OUR TOWN'S...

HEY, LOOK, SOME-THING'S COMING UP ON THE TV SCREEN AGAIN.
KCCCH

BWMM
RRRCH

WHO'S THAT?!

I'M THE LEADER OF THE RESISTANCE MOVEMENT IN THIS CITY. I'M GOING TO PLAY YOU A TAPE THAT WE GOT OUR HANDS ON...
RRCH
...OF A CONVER-SATION BETWEEN GOVERNOR JAGA AND WISE FROM THE ZENOM SYNDICATE.
WHAT...?
GYUGK
HERE'S THE MONEY FOR THE NEXT JOB.
THD
NO PROBLEM. I'LL DYE THIS TOWN IN CRIMSON ANY TIME YOU WANT ME TO.
ALL WE HAVE TO DO IS RETREAT WHEN YOU GUYS APPEAR. PIECE OF CAKE.
IT'S A TOUGH JOB, FORCING THE PUBLIC TO REALIZE HOW POWERFUL THE GOVERNMENT IS.
I CAN'T BELIEVE IT.
CLICK
AS YOU JUST HEARD, THE GOVERNMENT IS CONNECTED WITH THE ZENOM SYNDICATE.
THEY'VE BEEN DECEIVING US ALL ALONG.

MADO→
NOBODY'S EVER BEEN THERE TO PROTECT US.

AND THIS IS THE PRICE WE HAVE TO PAY FOR RUNNING AWAY—LOOKING DOWN AND RELYING UPON THE GOVERNMENT.

WE HAD TO PROTECT THIS TOWN WITH OUR OWN HANDS...
THAT'S RIGHT, TELL IT TO THEM.

A BOY IS FIGHTING THAT MONSTER ALL ALONE RIGHT NOW TO SAVE THIS TOWN. AND THAT BOY TOLD ME...

ZRCH

...THAT AS LONG AS WE KEEP CRYING AND RUNNING AWAY, WE'RE NEVER GOING TO BE ABLE TO CHANGE ANYTHING, AND NOTHING'S GOING TO CHANGE...
NO MATTER HOW LONG AGO IT MAY HAVE BEEN...
...I'M SURE YOU STILL REMEMBER THE BLUE SKY WE USED TO HAVE...
CRRCH

JIO...

EVERYBODY—
KEEP YOUR
HEADS UP HIGH
AND FIGHT!!!

AS YOUR LEADER, I ORDER ALL THE MEMBERS OF THE RESISTANCE MOVEMENT IN THIS TOWN—THAT MONSTER MAY HAVE STARTED MOVING, BUT IT ISN'T OVER YET.

COMMENCE FINAL OPERATION!! GOOD LUCK TO ALL OF YOU!!!

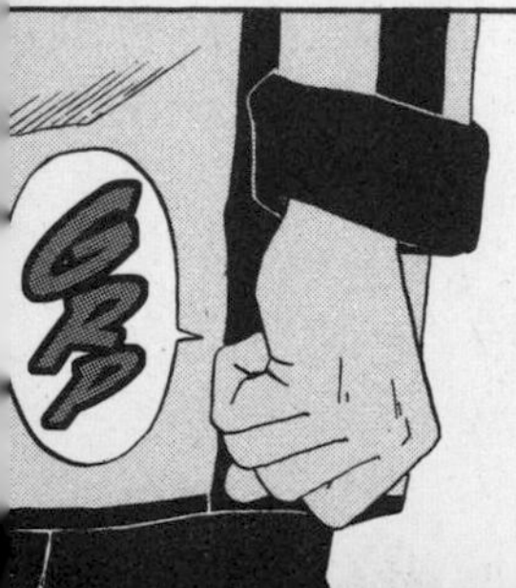

...WE'LL BE ABLE TO LOOK UP AT THE BLUE SKY ONCE AGAIN...

BLOCK A

HE'S PROBABLY GOT ANOTHER PLAN.
YEAH, IT'S A GOOD THING WE BELIEVED IN THE LEADER. WE'RE READY FOR ANY-THING!!!

SP
THIS'LL STOP ALL THE POWER IN BLOCK A.
I'M COUNT-ING ON EVERYONE IN THE OTHER BLOCKS.

CLICK
PHOOM

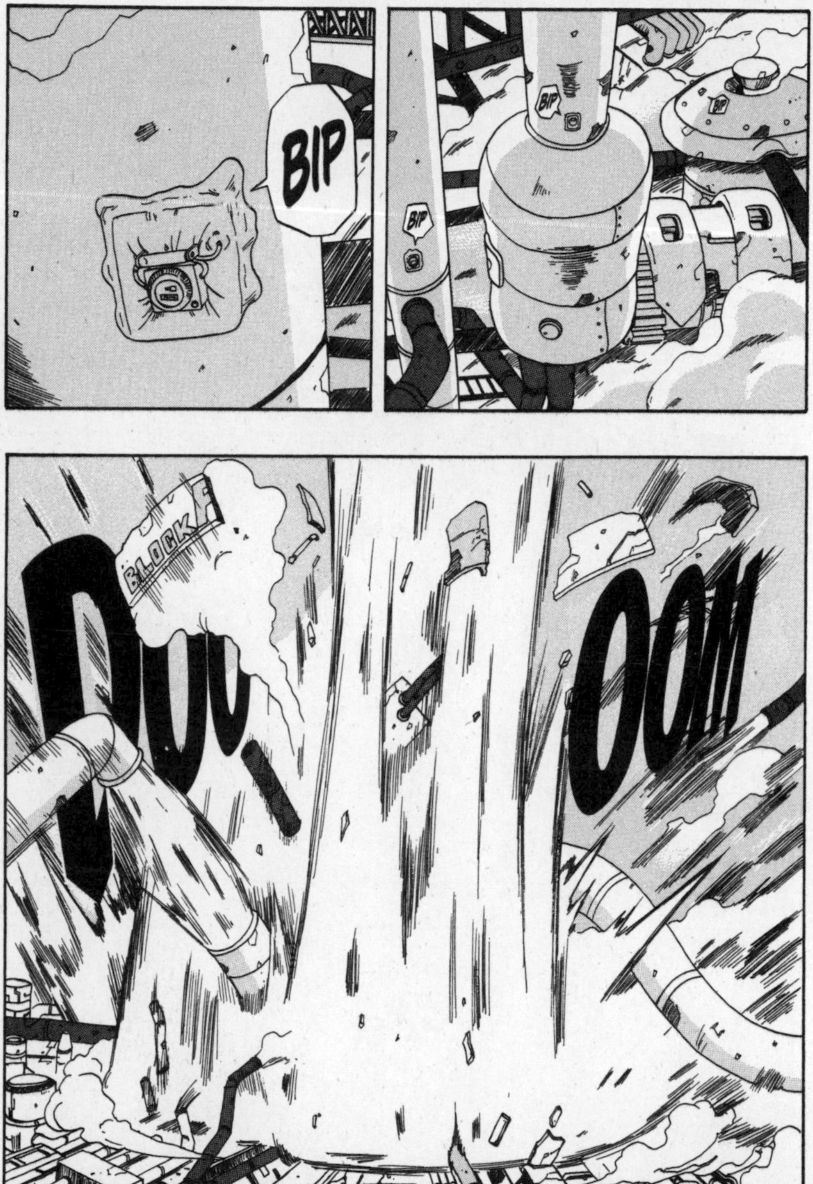

BLOCK
DOO
OOM

GSSSH

HSSS
HUFF
TCH.
HUFF

ZLLLLSH
THUD
WHOA.

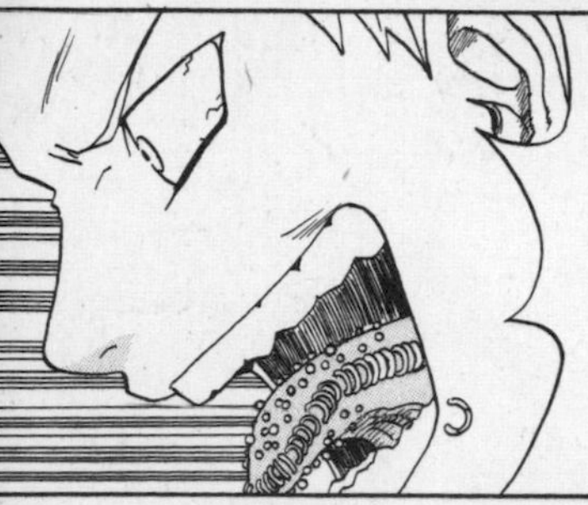

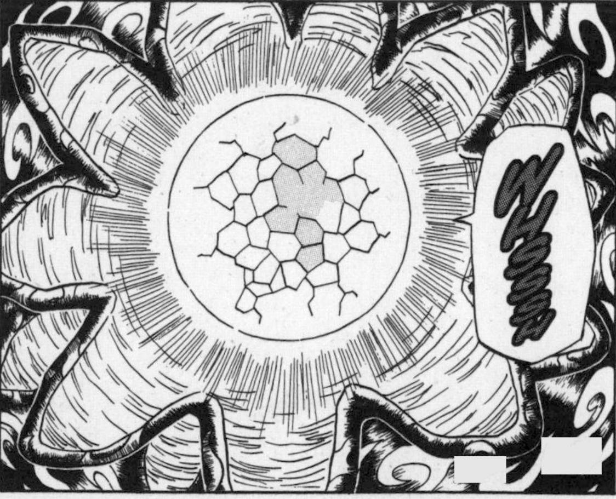

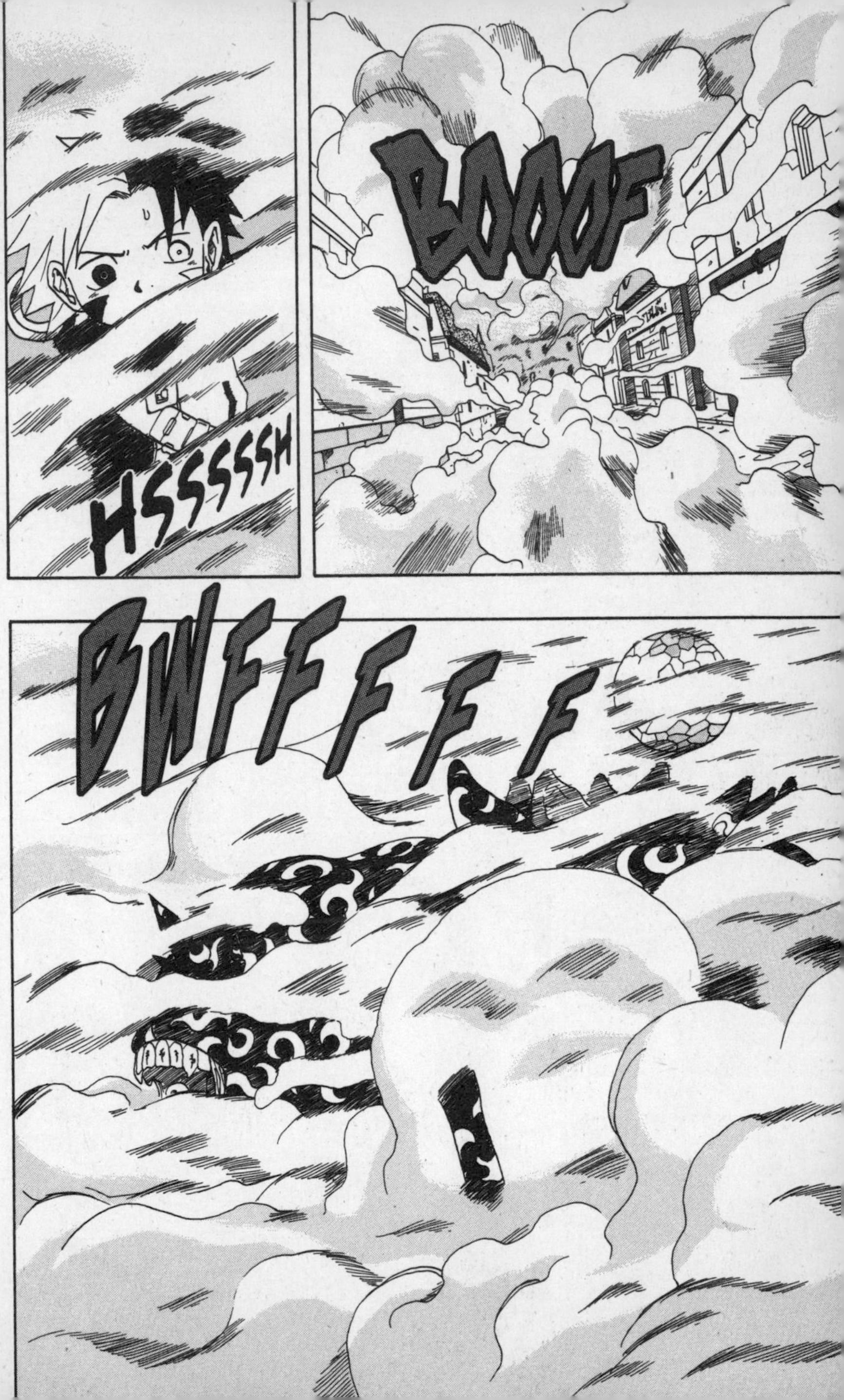

BOOOF
HSSSSSH
BWFFFFF

I SEE YOU, YOU PIECE OF SCUM. NOW DIE!!

SWWWW
SWWWSH!

WSH
WSH
WSH
VWOOOM
SZZZ
SZZZ
SZZZ
GOTCHA!!!

HUH, SO YOU GOT ME...

...BUT SO WHAT?

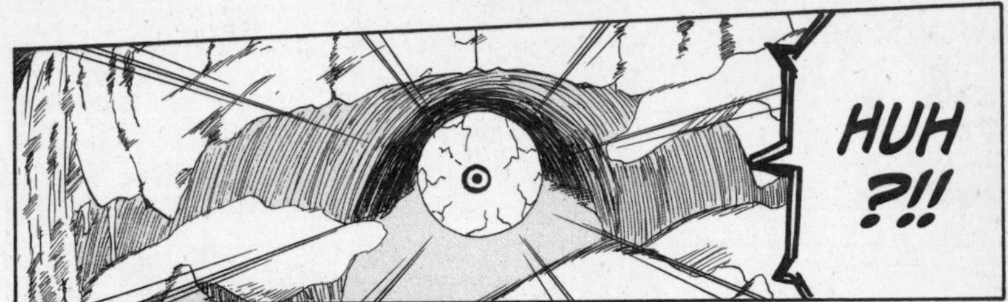

STEAM IS BASICALLY LIKE CLOUDS, SO IF THERE'S A LOT OF IT...
...IT INTERFERES WITH THE SATELLITE TRANSMISSION, AND IT DOESN'T LET SUNLIGHT THROUGH AS WELL.
HMM.

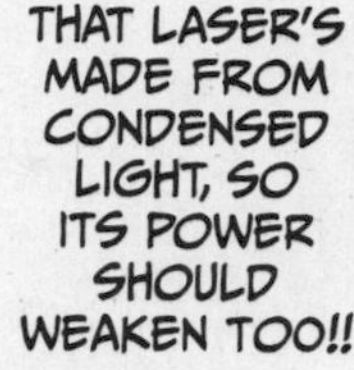
THAT LASER'S MADE FROM CONDENSED LIGHT, SO ITS POWER SHOULD WEAKEN TOO!!

TP
TP
TP
TP

BWIK
I... I CAN'T BELIEVE THAT THIS BRAT GOT THE BEST OF ME...
...AGAIN ...

IF THE LASER DOESN'T WORK, THEN I'LL JUST CRUSH YOU!!!

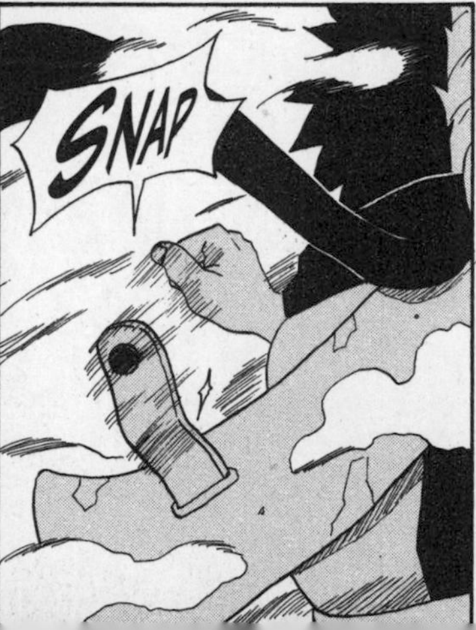
SNAP

GRAB
NOW...

...I'M CLOSE ENOUGH TO GET YOU!!!

KA CHAK

I'M GOING TO SLICE THAT HUGE LEG OF YOURS IN TWO!!!
BWMMM
RRRRSSH

BZZ
BZZ
BMP
!!

NO WAY... IT'S GOT A FORCE FIELD EFFECT TOO...

NICE TRY.
NOW WHAT ARE YOU GOING TO DO?

CHAPTER 21: EVERYBODY'S HEARTS AS ONE

PAP
SPNN
SPNN

A FORCE FIELD... HUH. SO THIS IS WHAT A HIGH RANKING O-PART IS LIKE...
KIRIN SAID IT WAS POSSIBLE TO DEFEAT A HIGH RANKING O-PART WITH A LOW RANKING ONE, BUT THE DIFFERENCE HERE IS TOO GREAT. WHA...WHAT AM I SUPPOSED TO DO?

TAKE THIS, YOU BRAT!!!

GITH

AAAH.
OU... OUCH.
WHAT'S WITH ALL THIS STEAM?! I CAN'T SEE ANYTHING!

HEY, RUBY. WHERE ARE YOU RUNNING OFF TO?!
TP TP TP TP
HUFF
HUFF
HUP
JIO'S OVER THERE!!

WAIT, RUBY. THAT MONSTER'S OVER THERE TOO.
YOU'RE GOING TO GET YOURSELF KILLED.
TP TP TP
TCH.
I'VE USED TOO MUCH SPIRIT TO RUN...
HUFF
HUFF

FWOOOSH
SHE SURE IS ONE TOUGH GIRL. SHE REMINDS ME OF YOU IN THE OLD DAYS, AMIDABA.
KIRIN!!
DO ME A FAVOR AND PROTECT THAT GIRL. SHE'S...
G G G G
YOUR REMAINING SPIRIT'S SEEPING OUT, YOU KNOW.
HUFF
HUFF
AAAH... OKAY, OKAY.
HUFF
HUFF

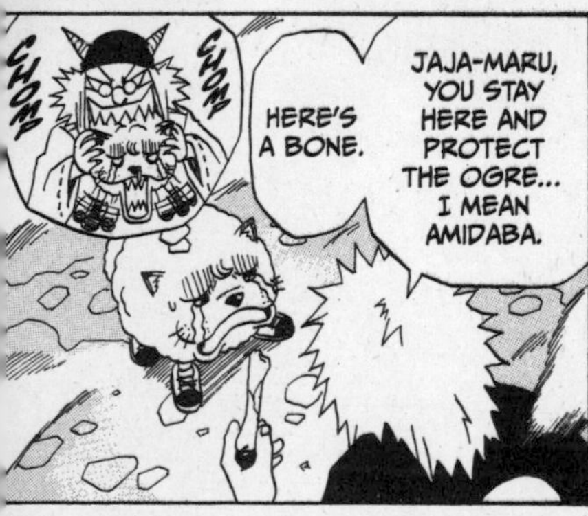

I'VE GOT SOME PERSONAL SCORES TO SETTLE WITH THAT MONSTER TOO.
TP TP TP TP
KIRIN ...
...TAKE CARE OF RUBY FOR ME...
HUFF
HUFF

WHA... WHAT IS THIS DENSE STEAM?!!
ALL THE POWER IS DOWN.
MAYBE THIS IS THE FINAL OPERATION THE RESISTANCE LEADER WAS TALKING ABOUT.

TWEEEE

NOW'S OUR CHANCE— WE CAN CONCEAL OURSELVES IN THIS STEAM AND GET BACK AT BOTH THE GOVERN-MENT AND THE ZENOM SYNDICATE.
WE KNOW MORE ABOUT THIS TOWN THEN ANY OF THEM.
LET'S DO IT.

THERE MUST BE SOME-THING WE CAN DO TOO.
THAT'S RIGHT. LET'S GET THE TOWN BACK TO THE WAY IT USED TO BE.

LEADER, EVERY-ONE'S GOT IT AT LAST.

EVERY-BODY...

!
KEEEE

TPTPTPTP

KE
TH... THE PENDANT'S GLOWING...

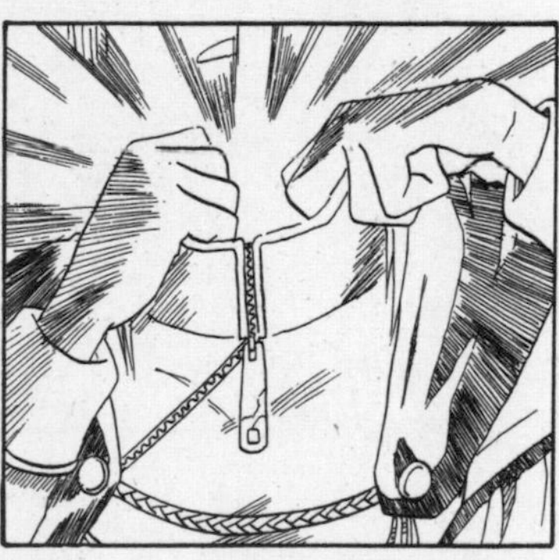

LOOKS LIKE THAT PENDANT'S BEGUN TO RESONATE WITH THE HUGE RESERVOIR OF ENERGY AROUND IT.

WHAT'S THIS? IT'S NEVER HAPPENED BEFORE...
KEEE

KIRIN!!

HUGE RESERVOIR OF ENERGY?
THAT'S RIGHT.

THIS IS ONLY SPECULATION, BUT IT COULD BE REACTING TO THE "MENTAL ENERGY" OF THE TOWNSFOLK.
THEIR STRONG FEELINGS OF HOPE ARE COMING TOGETHER AS ONE, AND TURNING INTO A HUGE POOL OF ENERGY.

THE PENDANT'S REACTING TO THAT AND ABSORBING IT.
THAT'S YOUR O-PART'S POWER. HOWEVER, THERE ARE A LOT OF THINGS WE DON'T FULLY UNDERSTAND ABOUT IT YET.

TRUST ME, I'M THE ONE WHO APPRAISED IT.

I HAVE TO HURRY.

YOU WANT TO HELP JIO, DON'T YOU?
H...
...HOW DO YOU KNOW JIO?!!

WELL, IT'S A LONG STORY...
FORTUNATELY, I'M NOT GOING TO STOP YOU LIKE AMIDABA.

LET'S GO, THEN.
YES!!

HSSSSSH

CRR

RSH

JIO
...

DAMN IT, IT'S A GOVERN-MENT OFFICER
...

TP TP TP TP TP
HUFF
RUBY!!

ARE YOU RUNNING AWAY FROM THE GOVERN-MENT?!
AND WHAT'S WITH THAT UNIFORM?
EH, WELL, I CAME DOWN HERE TO HELP YOU...
TP TP TP
HUFF
HUFF

YOU IDIOT!! WHY DID YOU HAVE TO COME DOWN HERE? YOU'RE ONLY GOING TO GET IN THE WAY!!!

HUFF
HUFF

HUFF
I JUST WANTED TO HELP YOU...
GRP
HUFF

YOU DIDN'T HAVE TO SAY THAT.
HUFF
STUPID JIO!!
HUFF

HUH?

HUFF
YOU'RE MY BODY-GUARD, AREN'T YOU? S... SO...
...YOU SHOULD PROTECT ME...

FOR GOD'S SAKE, GIRLS ARE SUCH A PAIN.
HUFF
AT ANY RATE, NOW ISN'T A GOOD TIME TO TALK!!
HUFF

JIO'S BEING BASHFUL.
YEAH, I AGREE.

YOUR FRIENDS, HUH?

NOTHING'S GOING TO CHANGE EVEN IF YOU GET HELP.
I'M GOING TO CRUSH...

...ALL OF YOU.

KIRIN, WHAT AM I SUPPOSED TO DO? THAT MONSTER'S GOT A FORCE FIELD EFFECT IN ADDITION TO THE LASER.
I CAN'T DO A THING TO IT.
THAT'S NO SURPRISE. A LOT OF THOSE HIGH RANKING O-PARTS HAVE FORCE FIELDS.

THAT'S RIGHT. THE SPIRIT OF HATRED! THE POWER OF EVIL!! THOSE ARE THE THINGS THAT TURNED MEXIS INTO ITS TRUE FORM AND FED ITS FORCE FIELD.
I SEE, SO THAT'S ITS ENERGY SOURCE.
IF YOU'RE USING THE POWER OF EVIL...

...THEN WE'LL JUST BREAK THROUGH IT WITH THE POWER OF GOOD.

VEEEEEE

IT'S GETTING BRIGHTER AND BRIGHTER.

RUBY, THROW YOUR PENDANT AT THAT MONSTER.
BUT...

DON'T WORRY, THAT PENDANT KNOWS WHO TO GO BACK TO.
I CAN TELL.

OKAY

SH-AA

I'M GOING TO DYE YOU CRIMSON!!

HE'S REALLY TRYING TO CRUSH ME THIS TIME!!

TH...THE SKY'S FALLING!!

HMM.

CRASH

HA HA HA. HA HA HA HA.
MEXIS, YOU'RE GREAT.

IT'S OVER... HE PLAYS AROUND WITH HIS VICTIMS AND THEN HE KILLS THEM...
HE SURE DOES LOVE TO TOY WITH PEOPLE'S LIVES.

NOW I GET TO ADD A FEW MORE PIERCINGS.
HAA...

I MIGHT NOT HAVE A FORCE FIELD, BUT AS LONG AS I'M NEAR THEM, NONE OF YOUR ATTACKS ARE GOING TO WORK.

HUH...

THE MONSTER'S FOOT IS RIGHT NEXT TO US...

WHAT?! THEY DODGED IT!!!!
IMPOS-SIBLE!!

WHO ARE YOU?!!
I DIDN'T THINK GUYS THIS TOUGH WERE STILL AROUND ...

I'M THE PERSON WHO HAD HIS PRECIOUS PICKLE JARS DESTROYED BY THIS MONSTER.
HURRY UP AND LET ME DOWN, KIRIN.

WHAT?! KIRIN?!!

THAT CAN'T BE TRUE— WHY IS HE... IN A PLACE LIKE THIS... BUT THAT SCAR ON HIS LEFT CHEEK, AND THE WAY HE DODGED MY ATTACK...
IF HE IS KIRIN, THEN HE'S MASTER KUJAKU'S ...

AH, SORRY, SORRY.
PA
TMP
OUCH!! DON'T JUST LET GO WITHOUT TELLING ME.

HEY, RUBY, NOW'S YOUR CHANCE.
OUCH ...
OH, RIGHT!!

HUH.

THIS LIGHT ...
...IS THE HEARTS OF EVERY-BODY IN THIS TOWN GATHERING AS ONE.

GRP

FWOOO
TAKE THIS!!

CRSH

AAAH.

NO WAY, THE FORCE FIELD EFFECT IS DISAP-PEARING!!
IT'S IMPOSSI-BLE!!

SSSSH

HSSSSH

WHAT'S GOING ON?!

BINGO!!
YEAH
HMM

THAT GUY CAN'T USE THE FORCE FIELD ANYMORE. NOW IT'S YOUR TURN TO DO THE BEST YOU CAN.
DO YOU REMEMBER HOW YOU'RE SUPPOSED TO USE YOUR SPIRIT?
REALLY ?
I DIDN'T GET WHAT WAS GOING ON, BUT IF THAT'S THE CASE, JUST WATCH.

I'LL DOUBLE, TRIPLE AND QUADRUPLE MY ATTACKS ON HIM.
CLAK

NOW!! I PUT ALL MY STRENGTH INTO THE O-PART RIGHT NOW—
BRRR
NOT...

Rssshh
RELEASE SPIRIT!!
O.P.T.: JIO

THAT BRAT, HE'S TOTALLY DIFFERENT FROM BEFORE
!!
...
LOOKS LIKE THE NEW ZERO-SHIKI CAN STILL TAKE IN MORE SPIRIT, BUT HE'S DOING FINE.
WELL DONE. HE'S NOT WASTING HIS POWER.
IS THAT REALLY JIO?!!
LOOK AT ALL THAT SPIRIT.

INITIATE EFFECT!!!
O-PART: NEW ZERO-SHIKI
O-PART RANK: B

SHOOM

EFFECT: TRIPLE (INCREASING POWER BY A FACTOR OF THREE)

SHHP

HUFF

GRAAA

I'M GOING TO EAT YOU.

GRAAA

HUFF

SLLLSH

SLLLSH

WHOA! IT'S ONE BAD THING AFTER ANOTHER! WHAT IS THAT THING?!!

JIO, WHAT'S GOING ON?!

VSH
GWOOP
TCH.
SQUISH

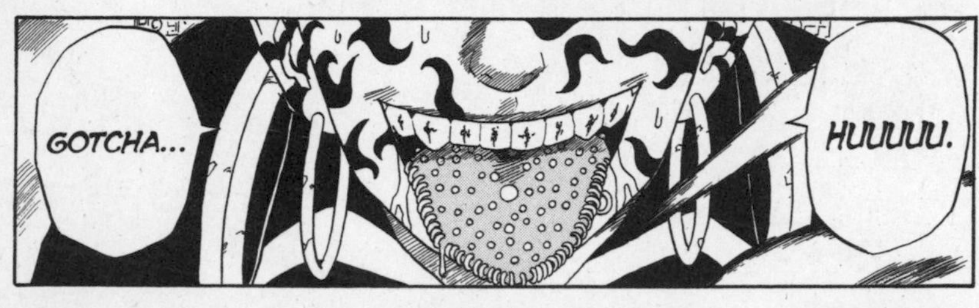

SSSSHHP

WHAT'S WRONG, JIO?!

GRP
SWSH

ZM
TCH, JIO'S INSIDE THAT THING... DAMN IT, HE'S TOO FAR AWAY FROM ME.

SLTH
SLTH

IT'S SO DARK ...
AM I DEAD ...?

CLINK

MONEY ...

RRRMMBB
UH...

AAAAH.

TH... THAT'S...

YOU'RE ...
...ALL ALONE ...

THOSE EYES!!

DMP
AH.

!!!

CHAPTER 22: A PACT WITH THE DEVIL

I'M YOU.
SHOOO

WHOA!!!

SATAN
...
VI6

SATAN?!! WHAT ARE YOU TALKING ABOUT...
WHAT DO YOU MEAN?!!

WHO ARE YOU CALLING SATAN?!
DAMN YOU, STOP JOKING!!!
...
VI6

I'M JIO!!!
JIO FREED— THAT'S WHO I AM!!!

Heh
YOU'VE JUST BEEN PRETENDING NOT TO NOTICE... RIGHT?
NO...

NO... I HAVEN'T DONE ANYTHING. I'M NOT THE ONE WHO MADE EVERYBODY UNHAPPY...
THAT'S A LIE. THIS IS JUST A DREAM. THE DREAM I HAVE ALL THE TIME...

UH...
IF THAT'S HOW YOU WANT TO THINK ABOUT IT, GO AHEAD.

TCH... WHY AM I SEEING THIS DREAM NOW...
I... I'M ME... I WON'T BELIEVE IT.

YOUR BODY...THE VESSEL IS READY.
MY BODY...A VESSEL?!

WHAT ARE YOU GOING TO DO WITH MY BODY?! YOU BASTAR—
I CAN HEAR YOUR HEART SAYING THAT YOU DON'T WANT TO DIE...

THAT YOU DON'T WANT TO BE ALONE...
SO... I'M GOING TO LEND YOU A HAND.

ACCEPT ME!!!

ACCEPT ME!!

RAISE YOUR LEFT HAND.
ZWA

SP

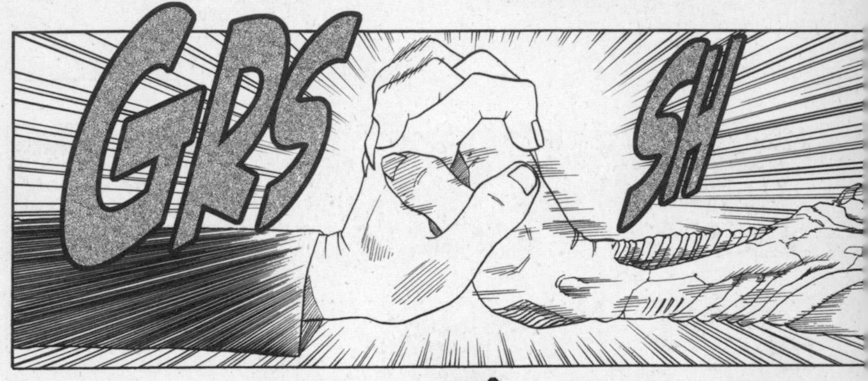
SH
GRS

!!!
SHWOOO
BMMM
BMMM
AAA-RGH!!!

SHUU
AAAAAAAAAARGH!

YOU'RE ALL ALONE.
HUFF
HUFF
IT'S... THAT DREAM AGAIN... B...BUT IT SEEMED SO MUCH CLEARER TODAY...
HUFF
HUFF
HUFF

O-PART: SHIN
RANK: SS

RRRMMBB

107
WH... WHERE ARE WE GOING...? URGH...
HUFF
HUFF

PSSSH

MY MY, COM-MANDER IN CHIEF, I SEE THAT YOU'VE WOKEN UP.

MAYBE YOU HAD A NIGHT-MARE? BRAT...
PSHHT
HUFF
HUFF

WE'RE CURRENTLY HEADED FOR ENTOTSU CITY, WHICH IS UNDER THE CONTROL OF THE STEA GOVERN-MENT.
WE'VE RECEIVED A CODE-RED NOTIFICA-TION.

HUFF
HUFF

GP

SATAN !!

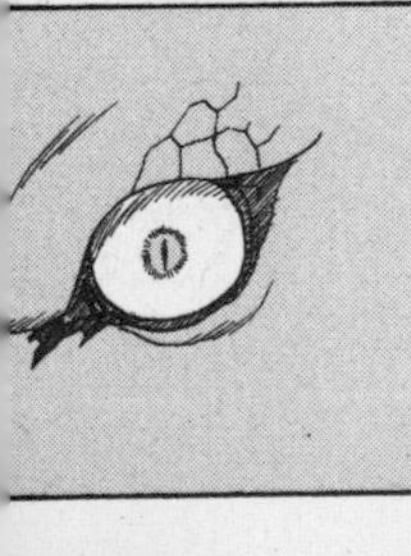

DAMN IT! WHAT DID YOU DO TO MY BODY!!!
IT HURTS LIKE HELL ...
WE'VE MADE A DEAL...
TAKE A LOOK AT YOUR LEFT HAND.

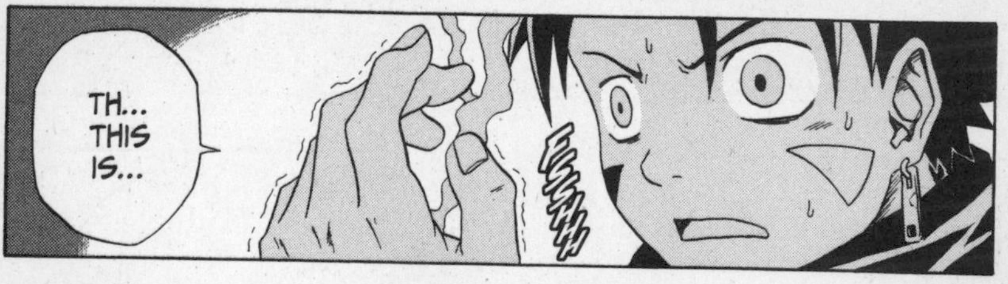
TH... THIS IS...

THAT IS MY MARK.
IT'S THE SYMBOL OF MY POWER.
SWP
VPP

YOUR POWER ...?

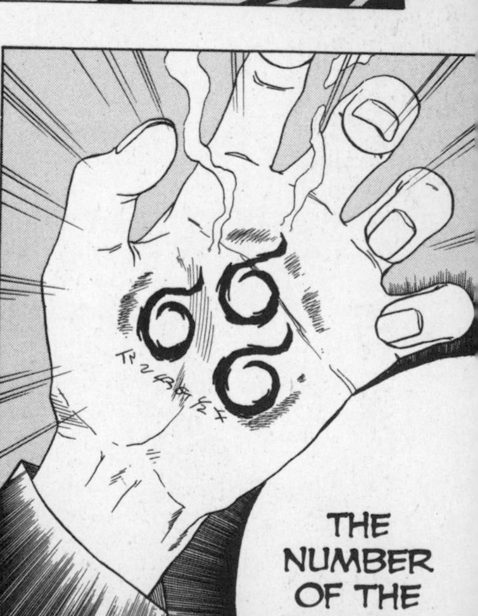
THE NUMBER OF THE BEAST-666.

M...MY LEFT HAND CAN USE AN EFFECT NOW...?

YOUR LEFT HAND IS NOW AN O-PART.

ENERGY ABSORP-TION.

...FOR YOU TO AWAKEN FROM THIS DREAM.

RRR MMM BBB

GUUUAH

WHA...
...WHAT IS... THIS FEELING ...?!

WHAT IS THIS? I SUDDENLY FEEL A STRANGE CHILL AROUND ME.

TH... THIS FEELING ...

GGGG

DOOOSH
THERE'S... NO DOUBT ABOUT IT...

RRRMMMBB
SATAN!!!

SO THIS IS IT, HUH?

SHOOOO
SPLKK
URGH!!!

SHP
SHP
!!!
BB
TH... THE MONSTER'S ...
... FLOAT-ING...
!!
WARGH

SHAK

DAMN, WHAT IS THAT THING?! I'M GOING TO HAVE TO DISCONNECT MY NERVES FROM MEXIS...

悪魔の刑(デビルペナルティ)
DEVIL PENALTY
FSH

ZDDSSH

SP
TCH, THAT WAS CLOSE ...

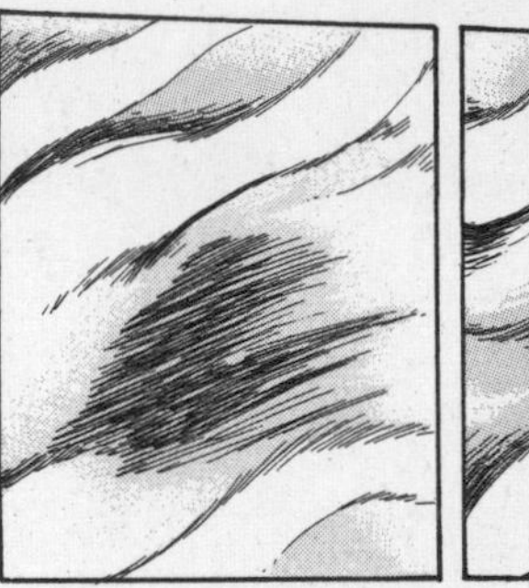

HE MUST HAVE FALLEN. TOUGH LUCK.

SLOSH
SLOSH

BROWNY ...

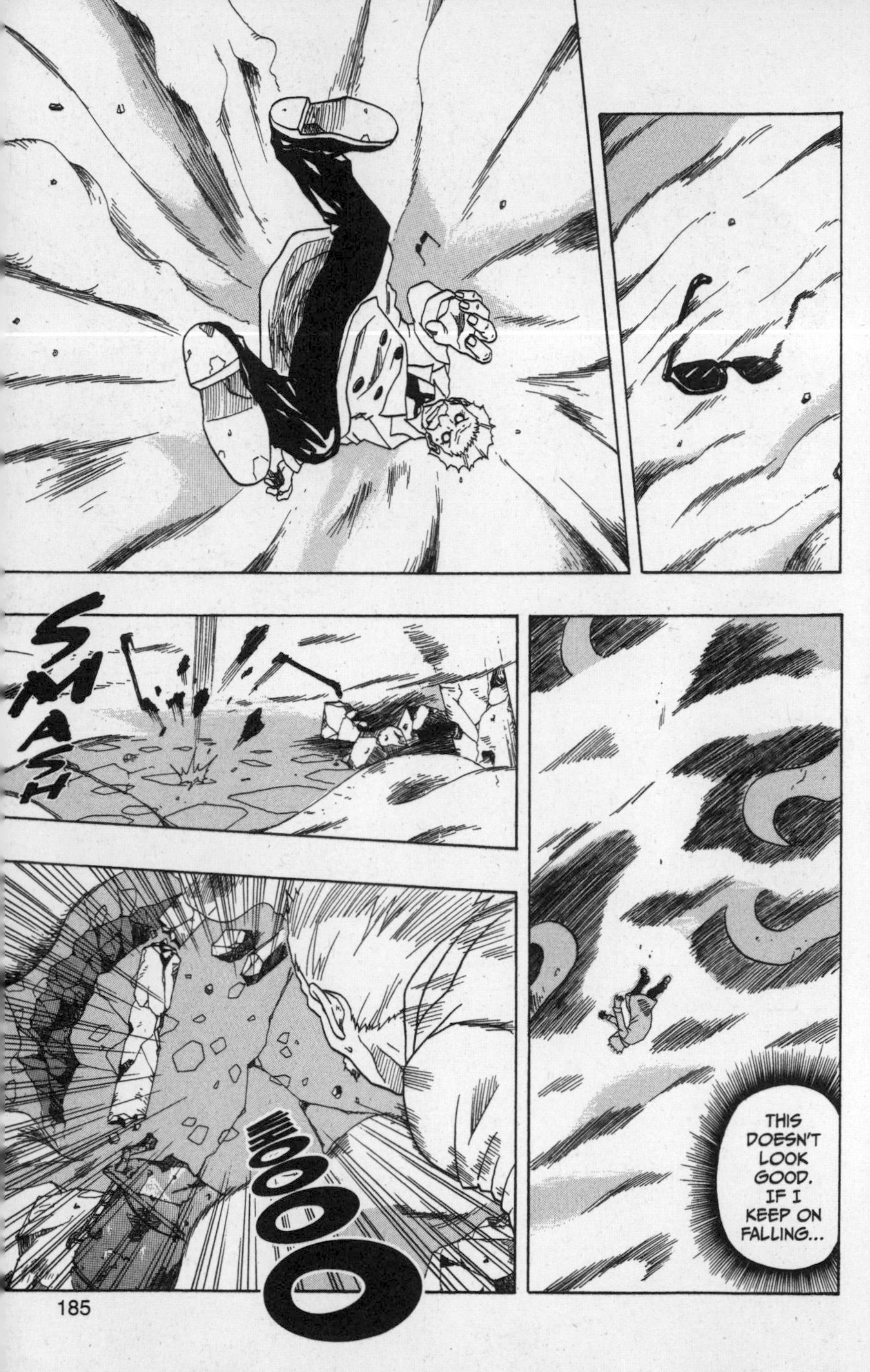
SMASH
THIS DOESN'T LOOK GOOD. IF I KEEP ON FALLING...
WHOOOOO

KKCCHH
SWISH

TH UD
URK
KKCCH

PWIK
KRCCHH
KRCCHH
WOBBLE
WOBBLE

O.P.T.: SHURI
(ZENOM SYNDICATE)

O-PART: WRAITH
O-PART RANK: B
EFFECT: ??

THAT BODY CAN'T BE USED ANYMORE, DR. BROWNY.

THERE REALLY WASN'T ANY OTHER WAY TO PROTECT YOUR HEAD.
SORRY.
SP
KCH
KCH
NO PROBLEM. I'VE GOT MANY MORE BODIES.

ALL THE DATA FOR THE SPIRIT DRIVE IS KEPT INSIDE MY HEAD TOO.
BAKU CONTACTED ME. THINGS TEND TO GET RATHER OUT OF HAND WHEN WISE TAKES OVER...
WE'VE GOT NO NEED FOR THIS TOWN ANYMORE. I'LL RETRIEVE YOUR HEAD AND GET OUT OF THIS PLACE.
I'VE HEARD THAT "SEVEN COLORED AMIDABA" HAS SNEAKED INTO THIS TOWN TO GATHER INFORMATION ON THE SPIRIT DRIVE.

SHUUUU
AT ANY RATE, WHAT IS THAT MONSTER... IS IT THE BRAT OR... WHAT'S GOING ON?
CAN THAT HAVE SOME-THING TO DO WITH KABBALAH TOO...?
TO BE CONTINUED!

SEISHI AND THE COMING-OF-AGE CEREMONY

SEISHI AND THE TAXI

O-Parts CATALOGUE⑤

O-PART: MEXIS 3RD FORM (PERFECT FORM)
O-PART RANK: S
EFFECT: LASER, FORCE FIELD
THOUGH IT IS NOT AN EFFECT, THE TOUGH BODY AND LEGS (TENTACLES) OF ITS 2ND FORM ARE MORE THAN ENOUGH TO DO MASSIVE AMOUNTS OF DAMAGE.

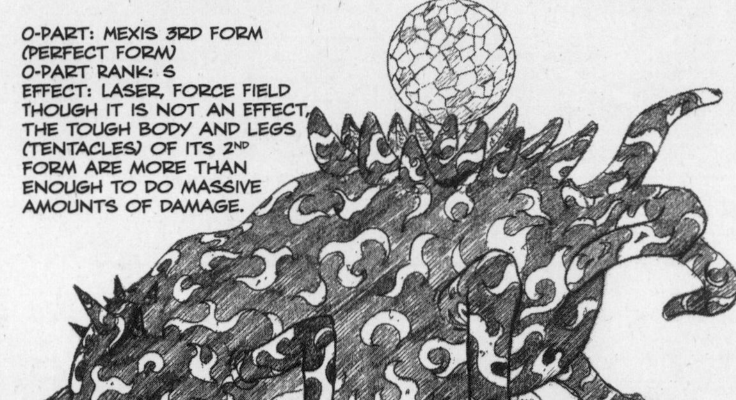

O-PART: LAVIAN
O-PART RANK: C
EFFECT: HEAT
THE O-PART WHICH THE TRIO FROM ZENOM HAD WITH THEM. IT'S JUST POWERFUL ENOUGH TO LEAVE A BURN MARK WHERE IT CUTS SOMETHING. RANK-WISE IT'S A LOW C.

O-PART: NUMBER OF THE BEAST (SATAN)
O-PART RANK: ?
EFFECT: ENERGY ABSORPTION, ?
HOLDS A TREMENDOUS AMOUNT OF DARK ENERGY. I CAN'T SAY ANY MORE ABOUT IT.

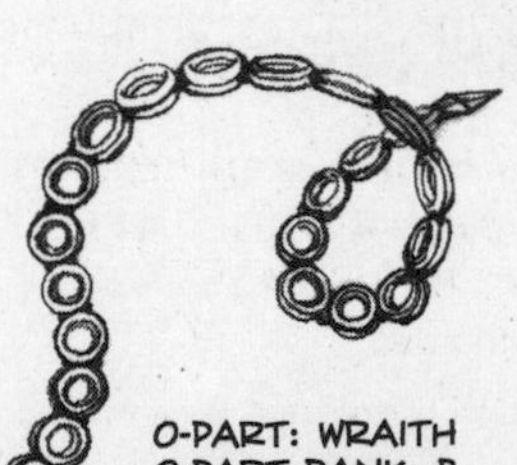

O-PART: HANG & TOOTH HANG
O-PART RANK: C
EFFECT: ALTERATION OF PHYSICAL MATTER. THE CLAWS AND FANGS USED BY MUSESHI FROM THE ZENOM SYNDICATE. THEY'RE EXTREMELY SHARP AND ARE EVEN ABLE TO SLICE THROUGH BONES.

O-PART: WRAITH
O-PART RANK: B
EFFECT: ?, ?
THE O-PART USED BY SHURI FROM THE ZENOM SYNDICATE...

SEISHI KISHIMOTO

I've recently begun to eat breakfast every day and my body feels a lot better!! Do you eat breakfast on a regular basis?

VIZ Media Edition
STORY AND ART BY SEISHI KISHIMOTO

English Adaptation/Tetsuichiro Miyaki
Touch-up Art & Lettering/Gia Cam Luc
Design/Amy Martin
Editor/Kit Fox

Editor in Chief, Books/Alvin Lu
Editor in Chief, Magazines/Marc Weidenbaum
VP of Publishing Licensing/Rika Inouye
VP of Sales/Gonzalo Ferreyra
Sr. VP of Marketing/Liza Coppola
Publisher/Hyoe Narita

Printed in the U.S.A.

Published by VIZ Media, LLC
P.O. Box 77010
San Francisco, CA 94107

10 9 8 7 6 5 4 3 2 1
First printing, August 2007

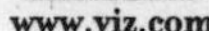

Become Part of the Legend
Join the Elric brothers' search for the mythical Philosopher's Stone with *Fullmetal Alchemist* manga and fiction—buy yours today!
viz media
www.viz.com
© Hiromu Arakawa/SQUARE ENIX
© Hiromu Arakawa, Makoto Inoue/SQUARE ENIX